What is
is
Unity?

What is Unity?

A View from
Chiara Lubich's Paradise '49

Edited by
Stefan Tobler and Judith Povilus

NEW CITY PRESS

Published in the United States by New City Press
202 Comforter Blvd., Hyde Park, NY 12530
© 2023, New City, UK (English translation)

Translated from the original Italian
L'unità, uno sguardo dal Paradiso '49 di Chiara Lubich
© 2021, Città Nuova Editrice, Rome

Translated by
Catherine Belzug, Bill Harnett, Thérèse Henderson,
Tim King, Brendan Leahy, Keith Linard,
Juanita Majury, Paul O'Hara, Judith Povilus,
Brendan Purcel, Barry Redmond, Callan Slipper

Cover design by Maria Oswalt
Layout by Miguel Tejerina

ISBN 978-1-56548-565-5 (paperback)
ISBN 978-1-56548-567-9 (e-book)

Library of Congress Control Number: 2023938154

Printed in the United States of America

Contents

Introduction
by Fabio Ciardi 9

Part One

The Foundations

1.– God's Project and Humankind's Searching.
The Charism of Unity and Biblical Revelation
by Giovanna M. Porrino 21

The Lord: The One God, the God of Tenderness 23

Man and Woman's Call to Be One Body 25

God of the Covenant 26

Babel and Jerusalem, from Uniformity to Unity 28

The Suffering Servant and His Mission 30

Fulfillment in Jesus 31

Unity Builders 33

Conclusion - Unity, Gift from the Holy Spirit 34

2.– The Roots of Unity
in the Experience and Thought of Chiara Lubich
by Stefan Tobler 36

The Call to Unity 38

The Book of Light: Unity and Jesus Forsaken 40

Turned toward the Father 44

My True Self 49

Jesus Forsaken: the Nothingness-all of Love 54

A Passion for the World 57

Part Two
Further Insights

3.– Unity and Diversity.
The Experience of the Soul
by Lucia Abignente, Stefan Tobler and Hubertus Blaumeiser 63

In the Early Years of the Movement 64
The Experience of the Soul in Paradise '49 72
1950 and the Transition to Everyday Life 81

4.– United in the Name of Jesus.
Unity and Nothingness in Interpersonal Relationships in Christ
by Brendan Leahy and Judith Povilus 88

A Robust Requirement of Love, Within the Reach of All 91
Living Nothingness in Order to have Jesus Among Us.
False Interpretations 94
A Positive Approach to the Ascetic Radical Nature of Love 99
The Realization of One's Personality 102
A Personal and Communal Ascetic Dimension,
a Mysticism of the New Commandment 105
Conclusion 107

5.– Freedom and Obedience in the Dynamics of Unity
by Anna Maria Rossi and Hubertus Blaumeiser 109

From Obedience to Unity 113
Freedom and Obedience in Unity 117
An Obedience which Generates 124
The Positive Pole and Negative Pole in Unity.
Light that Comes from the Night of God 128
The Vow of Obedience 133
Conclusion 135

6.– Chiara Lubich
   Mediator of a Charism for Unity
   by Fabio Ciardi 136

   Unity, the Fruit of a Charism 137
   Bearer of the Charism of Unity 140
   An Instrument of Unity 146
   Instrument of Unity for Humanity 153

List of Contributors 155

Introduction

by Fabio Ciardi

Unity!
But who would dare speak of it?
It's as ineffable as God![1]

It is not easy to talk about unity. The reality of the world around us and that of our own personal experience can often seem quite far from what the word "unity" promises. Unity, however, is an innate longing within the heart of every human being. Unity is a key theme in philosophy, it's central to the practice of politics, and it's at the heart of our everyday life with each other.

Talking about unity always involves a risk, because unity is something that transcends us and is *ineffable*. We are called to unity and tend toward it. The biblical story of our origins talks about a cosmos that God created beautiful and good, drawing it out of chaos and filling it with harmony. It speaks to us of a God who shaped Adam from the dust of the ground and breathed into his nostrils the breath of life, positioning him in unity with woman as well as with the created and the uncreated universe. God entrusted God's work to man and woman so that they might watch over it and accompany it throughout the course of history in its constant tendency toward unity.

The biblical narrative also tells of a collapse in that original harmony: first, in the relationship with God, then in a series of breakdowns between humankind and the natural

---

1. Chiara Lubich, *Early Letters: At the Origins of a New Spirituality,* New York 2012, p. 103.

world. A future is described: human beings working with the sweat of their brow; the earth producing thorns and thistles that would also produce suffering; motherhood becoming a source of pain for women; the man and the woman blaming each other, resulting in a breakdown of their relationship. We also read of how Lamec marries two women, tearing apart the unity of the family; Babel marks the splintering and misunderstanding among people.... And yet, the more distant unity becomes, the more the desire for that primordial harmony increases; the nostalgia for a distant past is coupled with striving towards a new future.

Unity is *ineffable*. Not only because of the inadequacy of language, which is never able to express such a big reality, a reality as great as God, but also because the very idea of unity is multifaceted. Its implementation has many expressions that are both simple and complex, so often beyond our human ability to define.

We all know of grotesque distortions of unity. Such distortions arouse fear. Sometimes they are associated with an official rigid model of unity. There is a fear of a unity that would lead to uniformity and ignore the creative richness of pluralism. Unity in a rigid uniform sense would seem to contradict the equally innate aspiration for freedom. Does the affirmation of identity and diversity contradict unity? Or is it an integral part of unity? It is interesting to compare Babel and Jerusalem. The dispersion of languages in the city of Babel produced a multiplicity of peoples whereas Pentecost in the city of Jerusalem brought about a convergence of different languages.

The two drives (toward unity; toward pluralism) which could seem to be in conflict with one another, are still with us and very much alive in today's world. For instance, in the last century we saw contradictory phenomena. On the one hand, we witnessed progressive political and economic regimes, various forms of socialism, the establishment of the United

Nations, the European Union and the Unions of African and South American countries, the World Trade and Health organizations... On the other hand, however, there was no lack of extreme nationalisms resulting in catastrophic wars whose wounds have not gone away in regimes repressive of pluralism of thought and of government.

History repeats itself today but in a new way, with new challenges. We wander between forms of globalization and yearnings for autonomy, between outbursts of fraternity that push toward reciprocal integration and veins of subtle anarchy that shy away from any form of structured organization.

Unity attracts us because it is inscribed in the very fiber of our being. But it also provokes fear because of the misconceptions that have led to constraining and authoritarian deviations that have been presented under the name of unity.

Chiara Lubich lived in the midst of such tensions in the Italy of her day, tensions experienced also in her own city of Trent: from the irredentism of her fellow Trent citizen, Cesare Battisti, to the socialist ideals of her father, from the Fascist action squads to the nationalisms of the Second World War, from the appeals of Pope Pius XII for a more united Christian society, to the birth of a new fermenting of charisms in the ecclesial world....

It was in the midst of such tensions that she proclaimed unity. She was well aware of the ambiguous interpretations that this word could arouse, but, for her, unity was something that demands our attention because the Gospel underlines it so much. It wasn't that she herself simply proposed to heal the many tensions and divisions of her times, nor those that were already looming on future horizons. It was not she who chose to make unity her ideal in life, but quite the opposite: It was the ideal of unity that chose her as its instrument for a new and creative way of living out the prayer with which Jesus took his leave of this world (Jn 17). This was a task that she had received and perhaps she too, like the prophet Jeremiah, would have said: "O Lord, you have enticed me, and I was enticed; you have overpowered me, and you have prevailed. If I say, 'I will not mention him, or speak any more in his name,' then within me there is something like a burning fire shut up in my bones; I am weary with holding it in, and I cannot" (Jer 20:7 and 9).

Unity appeared strikingly evident to Chiara;[2] she held fast to it and soon discovered the way to pursue it. Even then it remained *ineffable*. The sentence quoted at the beginning of this introduction is dated 29 April 1948: "Unity! / But who would dare speak of it? /It's as ineffable as God."

A year later, beginning on 16 July 1949, that unity, which she had begun to experience during the previous years, now opened up to a deeper understanding. While remaining ineffable, it became say-able, not because Chiara Lubich was capable of saying it, but because she had been told, and so could now retell. It was a period known in the Focolare Movement as "Paradise '49" (*P'49*), an intense mystical experience that was lived as a body with her first companions in the midst of the daily events of a summer break in the Dolomite Mountains. The experience continued for about two more years in the cities of Trent and Rome.[3]

It was not only a new knowledge about unity, but an event of unity, an experience that from that moment on would illuminate Chiara's life and the lives of many people with whom she shared what she had understood in that experience of light. "We had the impression," Chiara later wrote, "that the Lord opened the eyes of our souls to the kingdom

---

2. This book will often refer to Chiara Lubich simply as "Chiara." This decision not only reflects the familiar way that the members of the Focolare Movement referred to her, but it also conforms to the way that Chiara was addressed by personalities from the religious world and beyond, as well as by the general public.

3. The beginnings of this period of special graces is described in broad terms in the chapter by Stefan Tobler entitled, "The Roots of Unity in the Experience and Thought of Chiara Lubich" (pages 44 to 49).

of God that was among us, the Trinity indwelling in a cell of the mystical body."[4]

This event, which first involved only a small group of young women, gradually indicated a way that was destined to involve more and more people, and to become a key for understanding everything, to the point that Chiara was convinced that "the created things of the universe are on a march towards unity, towards God."[5]

This book finds its inspiration in that experience. Chiara Lubich communicated her experience in her collection of "Paradise '49" (*P'49*) writings which she constantly drew upon in the development of her spirituality and of her thought.[6] The experience has become the vibrant heritage of the Focolare Movement that Chiara founded and that continues to inspire many people today. To the "Abba School"—a cultural cenacle that she gathered around her when she was alive and that has continued after her death—she entrusted the task of studying the Paradise '49 writings in order to draw out the doctrine that is contained in them.[7] We are just at the beginning of this work, even though a number of studies have already been published in Italian.

---

4. Chiara Lubich, *May They All Be One*, London 1977, p. 44.
5. This is how it appears in a 1950 text without a more precise date: *P'49*, 1217. In this book, citations taken from the Paradise '49 manuscript will have as bibliographic reference the abbreviation *P'49* and the paragraph number, according to the numbering established by the author, followed by the date of that text where it is known. When dealing with a commentary note added by Chiara Lubich in the context of the Abba School, reference will be made to the note number and the number of the paragraph to which it belongs.
6. The collection of texts entitled *Paradise '49* has not yet been fully published. Many passages have been reported and analyzed in articles, especially in the *Nuova Umanità* Review, and in the publications of the Abba School's Studies Series.
7. The Abba School began in 1990. After Chiara's death in 2008 it has continued its work under the direction of the president of the Focolare Movement. It is currently composed of 24 members from different countries, representing 22 academic fields. They in turn are linked to a group of some 200 scholars who collaborate with them in research and study.

The hundredth anniversary of Chiara Lubich's birth provided us with the perfect opportunity to address one of the central themes of her charism; indeed, the very heart of her charism, as she repeatedly said: "Unity is our specific vocation. Unity is what characterizes the Focolare Movement";[8] "Unity, therefore, is our ideal and nothing else."[9]

Since unity is what characterizes the Focolare Movement, it is fitting that a few years after the death of its foundress the Movement is called to question itself regarding the inheritance and the mission that she bequeathed to it. It's a time to look at ways in which the Movement can continue to develop in a manner that is both creative and faithful. How in today's world are we to live in focolare communities, in groups of Focolare members, in groups who live and share the "Word of Life"? How are we to proceed along the paths of courage and freedom, avoiding authoritarianism and individualism, and facilitating the full development of our personal gifts in the pursuit of common objectives?

Of course, Chiara Lubich's legacy is much more far-reaching than the Movement. Her vision of unity sheds light on the difficult pathways to be traveled as we navigate our ways in openness to diversity, safeguarding legitimate autonomy, searching for our identity while all the time accepting others, integrating them and sharing with them. Her vision pertains to the Church, but it also sheds light on relations among religions, and it also has something to say regarding the civic sphere in terms of relationships among individuals and groups, regions and nations....

The theme of unity, given its vastness, depth, and relevancy, lends itself to vast horizons of research. What is presented in this book is modest; it is only the beginning of a reflection on some of the pages of Paradise '49 directly relating

---

8. Chiara Lubich, *The Secret of Unity*, London 1997, p. 20.
9. Ibid., p. 37.

to the key-theme of unity. This book is not intended to be a comprehensive discussion about unity and its multiple implications for the different fields of thought and practice. Rather, the focus in this book is on unity in the experience lived by Chiara Lubich and the first group that gathered around her in the years between 1949 and 1951 within the horizon of Jesus's prayer, "... that they may all be one. As you, Father, are in me and I am in you, may they also be in us, so that the world may believe that you have sent me" (Jn 17:21). The contributors to this book have limited themselves to the study of and reflection on just a few of the pages written up during that period. They have pointed out some dimensions that resonated for them within their own academic or specialist interest. Though this book is certainly not a complete discussion on such a vast and demanding topic, nevertheless we nurture the hope that the fruit of our study, thanks to the texts that seem to us of extraordinary richness, may be of benefit to the reader and open a dialogue with people of different cultural backgrounds.

This book is the result of the sharing among the current members of the Abba School acting in accordance with the style that Chiara Lubich gave to the study group when she gathered with its first members. For two years we met on a monthly basis to read her writings from Paradise '49, paying special attention to the theme of unity. Several contributions emerged, some of which are presented in this book, while others will be published elsewhere. Each contribution was born from the communion and sharing that characterizes all of the work done by the Abba School. Each text was put before the group for evaluation, in an ongoing dialogue that enriched it with new and different perspectives. Therefore, while the texts carry the signatures of their individual authors and reflect their style, expertise, and methodology, they are also the fruit of the communion among the whole group. This way of working in unity carries with it a certain "gymnastics" that was not

always easy but very worthwhile! It was necessary to welcome
and understand each other's diversity, often far perhaps from
one's own way of thinking and expressing things. We come
from different countries, have different academic backgrounds,
and work in distinct fields with distinct methodologies. It was
an opportunity that we happily and confidently welcomed.

This book is divided into two parts. The first offers a
global view of the topic from a biblical and spiritual-theological
point of view, keeping in mind the prism of Chiara Lubich's
thought. The second proposes four in-depth analyses of the
theme, based on texts from Paradise '49. In this way, we are
taken back to the origins of the charism and its foundational
intuitions that can help us grasp the meaning that Chiara
gave to the word *unity* and what she means when she asks
that we live it.…

Since the language of Paradise '49 is predominantly
of a religious nature, we wondered how to write a transdis-
ciplinary book about such an ambiguous word like *unity,*
without running the risk of talking about different things
and mixing vocabularies. The question had to be asked: In
what sense does the study and the life of Paradise '49 offer
criteria that can serve as inspiration for those who operate
in society and for those who carry out research within their
own distinct fields of knowledge? As will be stated further
on, "Various social realities and indeed academic reflections
in various fields have emerged from this Movement defined
by its spirituality of 'unity.' There should exist therefore a
common denominator, a point of departure, a fixed point
that allows all, even among those working in different fields,
to be able to make their own the words of Chiara and say
'Unity is our vocation'—even if perhaps they do not speak
specifically of unity but express it in a language specific to
their own discipline."[10] This book offers only a few intuitions

---

10. See Stefan Tobler on p. 39 of this book.

in relation to some fields of knowledge that will then need to be further explored and developed.

The goal of this book is to take a look at unity from the standpoint of Paradise '49 and to invite the reader to enter along with us into this communion of life and of thought.

Part One

The Foundations

1.– God's Project and Humankind's Searching. The Charism of Unity and Biblical Revelation

by Giovanna M. Porrino

On a day long ago when the Second World War was raging, as bombs were falling all around them in their city of Trent, Chiara Lubich and a small group of her first companions took refuge in a dark shelter. With the light of a candle, the young women opened the Gospel at random and came upon Jesus' prayer in John 17. As they read those words, they felt deep within their hearts that they had been born for that prayer. Chiara described it like this:

> It was during the war. A few girls and I were in a dark place, maybe a cellar. We were reading Jesus' last will and testament (John 17) by the light of a candle. We read it all through with ease. One by one those difficult words seemed to be lit up. It seemed to us that we understood them. We felt, above all, that here was the Magna Carta of our new life… After a little while, when we became aware of the difficulty, if not the impossibility, of carrying out such a program, we felt urged to ask Jesus for the grace of teaching us how to live unity. Kneeling around an altar we offered our lives to him so that, if he wished, he could bring about unity. As far as we remember, it was the feast of Christ the King. We were struck by the words of the liturgy that day: "Ask of me, and I will make the nations your heritage, and the ends of the earth your possession" (Ps 2:8). We had faith and asked.

Chiara continues:

> Until all are one, those "all" that Jesus certainly
> intended, the Movement can have no respite. This
> is the end for which we were born, the purpose for
> which he brought us into being.[1]

Unity was always the main feature of Chiara's divine adventure
and that of the Focolare Movement as it reached the very ends
of the earth, one might say, as it spread to all five continents.
The genius of this woman, who marked the twentieth century
with a gift from the Spirit, is without doubt that she spent
her life in the service of unity and in fruitful dialogue with
people of different faiths and even with people who had no
religious reference point. Chiara says that unity is a divine
word whose source is in God. If the world lived unity, we
would see "families being rebuilt," factories "being turned into
oases of peace," parliaments being transformed into "places
of encounter" in view of the common good. "In short, we
would see the world become a better place, heaven coming
down to the earth as if by magic, the harmony of creation
becoming the backdrop for the harmony of human hearts."[2]
But this unity will not be achieved by human efforts alone;
it is always a gift that can only come from above.

Jesus's prayer in John 17 is a foundational text of Chiara
Lubich's charism, which she called the charism of unity. It
takes us to the very heart of the Gospel, and so it is natural
to ask what the Bible says about unity.[3] What was the path

---

1. Chiara Lubich, *The Secret of Unity*, pp. 21 and 26.

2. "Unity, a Divine Word," in Chiara Lubich, *Essential Writings*, Michel Vande-
   leene, Thomas Masters, Callan Slipper (eds.), New York 2007, p. 98.

3. On several occasions and in several articles, this issue has been explored from
   the perspective of the New Testament. In this presentation, I have chosen to
   focus on its understanding in various Old Testament texts. The authors of the
   Hebrew Bible offer a reflection and a vision that can open us to dialogue with
   the Jewish people. The biblical vision of the Old Testament also provides valid
   interpretations for understanding universal history.

that the biblical authors had to follow in order to reach the dizzying heights of Jesus's prayer for unity that is contained in the fourth Gospel?[4] This question leads us right back to sacred scripture for an answer, right back to the very first days, to the absolute beginning as found on the first pages of Genesis. In this brief presentation, therefore, I would like to describe, in broad detail, how the sacred writers reflected on what unity is. Their reflections were accompanied by their own experience of faith and by the inspiration of the Holy Spirit. Entering the pages of the Bible is always an exciting challenge, but given the brevity of this article, it will not be possible to explore the entire biblical landscape. We will, however, try to provide an overview, bringing out some of the salient aspects of this vein of gold that runs through the whole Bible, creating the path that leads to unity.

The Lord: The One God, the God of Tenderness

Who is the God of Israel whom Jesus addresses as *Abba* (Mk 14:36)? Who is this God who manifested himself as the living one, the eternal one, the most high—and who revealed his name to Moses?

The Shema Yisrael, the daily affirmation of their faith, which the Israelites have been reciting from time immemorial, proclaims:

---

4. First, it should be noted that the abstract term "unity" is very rare in Old Testament Hebrew. In Jer 48:7 and 1 Chr 12:18, we have the idea of union, association, community. The same term, used as an adverb, can be translated as "together," "vicariously," "all together" (1 Sam 11:11; 17: 10; 2 Sam 10:15; Is 27:4; Mic 2:12). Or in a temporal sense as "at the same time," "completely" (Is 42:14; Ps 33:15). In the New Testament, the Greek term *henótēs* is found only twice in the letter to the Ephesians (Eph 4:3, 13).

> *Hear, O Israel: The Lord is our God, the Lord alone.*
> *You shall love the Lord your God with all your heart,*
> *and with all your soul, and with all your might.*
> (Dt 6:4-5)

This Hebrew profession of faith affirms that the Lord is the only God, whose revealed name (YHWH) is never pronounced in the Jewish tradition, but substituted with the term *Adonai*, which means Lord. He is one (*œḥād*), which expresses his uniqueness and his fullness.

But who is this God that reveals himself in this way? To understand a bit of the mystery we can turn to a passage from the book of Exodus that describes God's manifestation to Moses, after Moses had dared to ask the Lord to let him see his glory. God passes by and Moses can only see him from behind. The light of the living God would be left on Moses's face which, from that moment, became radiant with light. As the Lord passed in front of the rocky ravine on which Moses was standing, God spoke some words that could be taken as a theological commentary on the message of the Shema:

> *The Lord descended in the cloud and stood with him and proclaimed the name, "The Lord." The Lord passed before him, and proclaimed, "The Lord, the Lord, a God merciful and gracious, slow to anger, and abounding in steadfast love and faithfulness, keeping steadfast love for the thousandth generation, forgiving iniquity and transgression and sin..." (Ex 34:5-7a)*

When Moses asked to see the glory of God, the Lord revealed God's invisible face: He is a God of goodness and mercy, slow to anger and rich in goodness for thousands of generations. The Lord manifests himself as *El raḥum*, that is, a God of tenderness. He is a God who loves with motherly love. And the word that expresses the deepest reality of God is *ahabā*, love. The *most* high who revealed his name to Moses is the only God and the one God, but also a tender, loving and faithful God. Being one/unique is one of the characteristics of the God of Israel, which closely combines with his tenderness, with his goodness, with his love for us. This is what Psalm 136 proclaims—which twenty-six times repeats that his love (*chesed* in Hebrew) endures forever. So we already have several Old Testament texts that suggest what John will later affirm in his first letter: "God is love!" (1 Jn 4:8-16).

Man and Woman's Call to Be One Body

After asking who the God of Israel is, we can now ask: Who or what are human beings? This is the great question of the psalmist who is confronted with the wonders of creation and feels compelled to ask God: "*What are human beings that you are mindful of them, mortals that you care for them?*" (Ps 8:4-5).

Harmony reigns in both creation stories.

In the first story, after having created the heavens and the earth, God creates humankind in his image and likeness (Gn 1:26-28 and 31): Humankind is created male and female and, together, they are the image and likeness of God. The creation of the first human couple is said by God himself to be very good. God blesses them, with a mandate to be fruitful and to inhabit the earth.

In the second creation story, a similar image underscores the unity of the first human couple, the plan of unity. Adam is created from the earth and receives the divine breath that makes him live. The woman, on the other hand, is taken from Adam's side. When God presents woman to man, Adam bursts into a cry of joy:

> *This at last is bone of my bones and flesh of my flesh;*
> *this one shall be called Woman ['iššāh], for out of*
> *Man ['îš] this one was taken.* (Gn 2:23-24)

Man (*adam*) acknowledges this (female) creature formed by God, as bone of his bones and flesh of his flesh. The woman is like a mirror for the man. He recognizes her and names her and sees himself in her. The first human couple, molded by the hands of the Lord, bear the mark of God the creator in the depths of their identity. The couple are the living icon of the God of life. The next verse reveals their call *to be one body.* The communion which they are called to incarnate will be fully manifested in the fruit of their love.[5] The original icon that emerges from the text is the image of a garden in which a man and a woman live united in the presence of God.

In this first human couple, the whole of humankind is called to be a family. But through disobedience to the divine command (Gn 3) this original unity is shattered. Man, woman and the whole of creation find themselves in a new state marked by disharmony and mistrust. The author of Genesis 2 and 3 suggests a break between the glorious condition of man and woman in the Garden of Eden, and the shameful and very fragile existence they will later have. The call to communion and unity, which characterized the original divine plan, turns into a reality marked by division and oppression.

God of the Covenant

In the language of the Bible, God's condescension takes the form of the covenant. Scripture tells us about the first covenant

---

5. Raschi, the great Jewish commentator from the Middle Ages, comments: "The child is created by the two parents, and it is in the child that they become one flesh."

between God and the human race at the moment of creation, but it also describes the break caused by the disobedience at the beginning. Once again, the Lord takes the initiative. He talks again with humankind and enters into several covenants with human beings. The term "covenant" (in Hebrew *berith*) appears for the first time at the conclusion of the story of the flood. God stipulates a covenant with Noah, a universal covenant, made with every living creature (Gn 9:9-17).

Then follows a specific covenant with Abraham, first sanctioned with a sacrifice (Gn 15) and then in the very flesh of the patriarch with circumcision (Gn 17), which will become the sign par excellence of the covenant with God for all of the Jewish people. The real covenant is stipulated at Sinai where the people, freed from Egyptian servitude, enter into a covenant with YHWH. The covenant that the Lord stipulates with the Israelites is not a covenant between equals but is analogous to the covenants of sovereignty: YHWH decides in his sovereign freedom to grant his covenant to Israel, who thus becomes his people and committed to respecting the words of the Lord.

The formula of the covenant, which is a recurring theme of the Hebrew Bible, states: *You will be my people, and I will be your God.*[6] But the message of the prophets is a constant denunciation of Israel's idolatrous infidelity to its God: the adulterous people do not respect the covenant, but worship other divinities. These messengers of the Lord look for new analogies drawn from human experience to express the covenant relationship of God with his people: Israel is the flock and YHWH the shepherd; Israel is the vineyard and YHWH the winemaker; Israel is the son and YHWH is the father; Israel is the bride and YHWH the bridegroom. All of these images, rooted in the Sinaitic covenant in God's gratuitous love for his people, are also beautiful metaphors to express *the relationship of love and communion* that God wishes to establish with the

---

6. Jer 31:33; 32: 38; Ez 36: 28; 37: 27.

Israelites and with all humankind. We should keep in mind that the prophets will strongly insist that the covenant with God also requires a commitment of love toward other human beings, toward the stranger, the least and the needy. Fidelity and love for God have always been intricately linked to fidelity and love of neighbor ever since the ancient covenant.

With a language that is rich in imagery, the prophets will deepen the doctrine of the covenant by also looking to the future: Israel has indeed broken the ancient covenant, but God always remains faithful to his promise. Prophetic preaching gives a glimpse of a new covenant on the horizon, an eternal covenant, a covenant of peace (Ez 16:60; 34:23; 36:26). The architect of this new covenant will be the mysterious servant whom YHWH will establish as *"the covenant of the people and light of the nations"* (Is 42: 6; 49:6). The plan of the covenant, which dominates human and biblical history, is now turned toward the future, toward the new covenant which will culminate in Jesus of Nazareth.

Babel and Jerusalem, from Uniformity to Unity

There are two cities in the Hebrew Bible that represent two different ways of achieving unity. In the city of Babel there is a unity that emerges from human desire and is dominated by uniformity. In the holy city of Jerusalem a pluralist unity emerges that is both desired and provided by God. Only God can reunite all peoples and languages, in peace.

Babel is the city of uniformity where a single, closed, standardized language is spoken. The socio-political plan of the citizens of Babel is to build a city with a tower that touches the sky in order to make a name for itself on earth and not be dispersed (Gn 11:3-4). Their dream is to gather and fix their home in a single place, imposing a single language and contravening God's command to inhabit the whole earth. It is a vainglorious project—*making a name for itself*—that does not take God's plans into account. The unity desired by the people of Babel leaves no room for relationships. The dispersion and multiplicity of languages willed by God opens up to plurality what otherwise is an unlivable uniformity. The theme developed in Genesis 11—albeit from a different time—expresses a desire to unite the human race in one socio-political center with a powerful government, one way of thinking, and one language that repeats the same words, even capturing heaven for its own political goals. But the unity that is willed by God has its source in the very rich diversity of languages and cultures, in a genuine and truthful dialogue that is based on love.

Jerusalem, on the other hand, appears as the anti-Babel. Despite its fragility and infidelity, it is the city chosen by God for his dwelling. In the second part of the book of Isaiah, Jerusalem appears as the center of the world, the center of a sacred cult that is open to all nations, the place where all the peoples of the earth will be gathered. Zion receives the promise of an unprecedented and endless fruitfulness and of a new offspring (Is 54:1-3). The city is invited to rejoice because the creator is her spouse (Is 54:5). The Lord (YHWH) is the bridegroom of the city and will make his wife Zion fruitful. In the concluding chapters of the prophet Isaiah, the city is invited to clothe itself with light and rejoice because the glory of the Lord will shine upon it (60: 1) and behold, nations will come to its light (60: 3-5). In Jerusalem, on the holy mountain, the Lord will gather all nations and all languages: "… and I am coming to gather all nations and tongues, and they shall come and shall see my glory" (66:18). In Jerusalem, God will gather all the peoples into his house, which will become a house of prayer for all peoples (56:7). Hence, the glory of Jerusalem will consist in being the mother of all nations (Ps 87). In Babel, God scattered the inhabitants of the city and multiplied the languages; in Jerusalem the Lord gathers all the peoples and languages. The centripetal force of Isaiah corresponds to the centrifugal force of the dispersion in Genesis 11. The work of gathering the missing will be carried out by the Spirit of the Lord, in the city of God. The forced unity of Babel fails to safeguard humankind from an exploitation that dehumanizes; the unity of Jerusalem is a gift that is welcomed by God and bears many fruits.

The grand eschatological vision of Isaiah will be taken up again, magnified and brought to fulfillment by the author of the final two chapters of the book of Revelation (Rev 21-22). The seer of the Apocalypse takes up the Isaian theme and also presents the city as the Lord's bride: *"And I saw the holy city, the new Jerusalem, coming down out of heaven from God, prepared as a bride adorned for her husband"* (Rev 21:2). God's marriage with humanity will be fulfilled in the heavenly Jerusalem.

The Suffering Servant and His Mission

In the second part of the book of Isaiah, the mysterious figure of a man appears, who is described in four poetic compositions known as the four "Songs of the Suffering Servant." In the first poem (Is 42:1-9), the Lord chooses the servant and establishes him as the covenant of the people and light of the nations (42:6). The servant's mission is to lead Jacob back to God and reunite Israel, but this is not enough. Precisely because he is the light of the nations, his task is to bring the salvation of the Lord to the ends of the earth (49:5-6). His mission, of cosmic dimensions, will be accomplished through a mysterious path of pain. The Servant will take "all our iniquities" upon himself (53:6). But after his torment and death, the Servant will give salvation, be lifted up and see the light. The prophet does not say how this will happen, but he traces out a future of light…

These texts are read in many Christian churches during the Easter Triduum. The primitive community had already interpreted the texts of Isaiah in the light of the passion, death and resurrection of the Nazarene. In the Gospels, Jesus is presented as the one who came to serve (Mk 10:45), who lives in the midst of his friends as "the one who serves" (Lk 22:27). In John, Jesus is twice designated as the lamb of God (Jn 1:29 and 36). This is a strong link with the suffering servant who, like a lamb, is humiliated and led to slaughter (Is 53:7). The evangelist speaks of Jesus' mission on earth: like the Isaian servant, he must "gather together the scattered children of God and make them one" (Jn 11:52). How will Christ accomplish this mission? By being lifted up on the cross: *"And I, when I am lifted up from the earth, will draw all people to myself"* (Jn 12: 32; 3:14; 8:28). The cross, a place of contempt and shame, becomes a place of transformation and salvation.

Fulfillment in Jesus

Christian faith identifies Isaiah's suffering servant with Jesus. The plan of salvation is fully accomplished in Jesus. At this point, having highlighted some aspects of the main theme of unity, we can begin to sense the depths of the prayer that Jesus addressed to the Father at the Last Supper as recounted in John's Gospel. In that moment when Jesus is preparing to leave the world and his disciples, he turns his entire being toward the Father in a prayer that expresses his deepest desire: the hour has come when the plan of love and truth that God has always wanted for humanity is fulfilled. The covenant with Noah, with Abraham and his descendants, the divine plan—it all culminates and is fulfilled in Jesus, engaging apostles, and disciples of the Nazarene in a slow transformation, the germination of a world renewed by love.

The prayer in John 17 culminates in this ardent plea to the Father: "… *that they may all be one. As you, Father, are in me*

and I am in you, may they also be in us" (Jn 17:11 and 21-23).[7]
Everybody's *being one* has its foundation in the *being one* of the
Father and the Son. There is a mutual immanence, an unpar-
alleled indwelling of the Father in the Son and of the Son in
the Father. The deepest calling of every Christian, and of every
human being, is this: to participate in the very life of God, in
the intimate relationship of the Son giving himself completely to
the Father and the Father giving himself completely to the Son.
Humankind is called to be "one" in the God of love. However,
entering into this ineffable communion, into the unity of the
Father and the Son, has a purpose: *"... so that the world may
know that you have sent me and have loved them even as you have
loved me"* (17:21). To be witnesses of trinitarian love is to bear
witness to the crucified-risen Christ, so that the world may
believe with a living faith which springs from *knowing* in the
fullest sense that this verb assumes in the Hebrew language of
the Bible; that is, a knowledge of love—that he is the one sent
by God. The prayer that Jesus addresses to his Father concludes
with this dense verse that summarizes it all:

> I in them and you in me
> that they may become completely one,
> so that the world may know that you have sent me
> and have loved them even as you have loved me.
> (17:23)

Furthermore, living in trinitarian communion is not only a
participation in the love-unity of God; it is also a sharing of joy,
being made participants of the fullness of joy (Jn 17:13) that can
only be given by Jesus (Jn 15:11). This gospel passage—which
gives us a glimpse of the intimate union of Jesus with the Father
and the calling of humankind to be one in God—was foundational in the life of Chiara Lubich. Reading this passage, as

---

7. The Greek text reads "perfectly one."

we recalled at the beginning of our journey through the Bible, aroused a passion for unity in those young women from Trent, along with the certainty that the Movement had been born for that prayer of Jesus to contribute to the unity of people with God and with each other.

Unity Builders

Let us return to that thread in the Bible which has led us to this point. In the second chapter of Acts, after having received the Spirit which Jesus had promised, the apostles and the first nucleus of the nascent Christian community boldly proclaimed the good news that "Christ is risen!" The crowd that had gathered and listened to their message was utterly amazed: *"Are not all these who are speaking Galileans? And how is it that we hear, each of us, in our own native language?"* (Acts 2:7-8). It is in their own language that these people, coming from many places, hear the wonders of God that are proclaimed by the apostles. Something completely unheard of is happening in the Lucan account: the Spirit re-establishes the unity of the languages that had been dispersed in the city of Babel, and in a completely new and unique way. The unity manifested at Pentecost is plural, and the plurality of languages is no longer an obstacle to unity. The outpouring of the Spirit in the upper room makes it clear that the unity willed by God integrates plurality. The loving will of the triune God brings many people together in unanimity, but unanimity is different from that single way of thinking that imposes itself, to the detriment of diversity. The unity willed by God flows from the depths of the Spirit of the Lord. A new centrifugal force begins again in Jerusalem: it is no longer the dispersion that took place in Babel, but a sending out on a mission of taking the good news to the ends of the earth.

A similar movement of proclamation went forth from Trent in the mid-twentieth century. Chiara described it in this way:

> Often, at the beginning, faced with the immensity of the task, we were overcome by dizziness and, seeing the crowds that we should help to gather into unity, we were taken aback. But slowly, the Lord gently made us understand that our task was like that of a child who throws a stone into the water. We could imagine larger and larger circles forming around the spot where that stone had landed. This made us think that we would have to create unity with the people around us, in the environments we were. Then, when we went to heaven, we would be able to watch the ever-widening circles, until the end of time and the fulfillment of God's plan. From the first moment it was clear to us that this unity had only one name: Jesus. For us, to be one meant to be Jesus, all of us together Jesus. In fact, only Christ can make two [people] one, because his love that is self-annihilation, which is not egoism, allows us to enter fully into the other people's hearts.

Conclusion
Unity, Gift from the Holy Spirit

Unity and communion are deeply instilled in God's creation, especially in the hearts of all human beings. Due to the original disobedience, this plan of God for humankind was in some way shattered, and man and woman found themselves in a condition of brokenness, shame, dispersion. The Bible tells us that the God of all tenderness has put a plan of salvation in place, which frees humankind from this bitter and opaque condition of being deprived of its original glory. This journey has been long and studded with many stages. The realization of God's plan, which opens to a horizon of light, is linked to the mysterious suffering of the servant of YHWH, that eschatological figure whom God himself establishes as the covenant and the light of the peoples.

Right from the start, Christians have found all of these promises and expectations to be realized in Jesus of Nazareth. His prayer for unity spans the centuries of human history until the end of time. It is always current and up-to-date and ready to be realized each day. Following the lamb that was slain, we are called, while walking around in a wounded world, to do everything we can to answer this prayer, remembering always that unity is a precious gift that can only be given by the Holy Spirit. Unity does not simply arise from the good will of human persons, nor from a desire for dialogue or some group dynamic. Unity is not an imaginary fusion of persons or human communities. Unity is a gift that flows from the perennial source of mutual love, which binds the Father and the Son in the Spirit. Unity requires deep adherence to the gospel message, bearing witness to the world that Jesus is risen, that he is alive among us forever in accordance with his promise: *"And remember, I am with you always, to the end of the age"* (Mt 28:20). It will be the unity of the disciples that will witness to the world the ineffable unity of the Father and the Son. Christians live in *the already* promised and *the not yet* of full unity, which will only be realized with the final coming of the heavenly Jerusalem, God's true dwelling with people: "See, the home of God is among mortals. He will dwell with them; they will be his peoples, and God himself will be with them" (Rv 21:3).

2.– The Roots of Unity in the Experience and Thought of Chiara Lubich

by Stefan Tobler

> This is the great attraction of modern times: to penetrate to the highest contemplation while mingling with everyone, one person alongside others.
>
> I would say even more: to lose oneself in the crowd in order to fill it with the divine, like a piece of bread dipped in wine.
>
> I would say even more: made sharers in God's plans for humanity, to embroider patterns of light on the crowd, and at the same time to share with our neighbor shame, hunger, troubles, brief joys.
>
> Because the attraction of our times, as of all times, is the highest conceivable expression of the human and the divine, Jesus and Mary: the Word of God, a carpenter's son; the Seat of Wisdom, a mother at home.[1]

This reflection is taken from the book of *Meditations* by Chiara Lubich, first published in Italian in 1959 and which since then has seen multiple editions.[2] It's a reflection that lays out her life's program and that of the Focolare Movement which she founded. To live in God and live in the world are not two different things. Jesus described the love of God and love of neighbor as intimately connected and Chiara saw this not only as an ethical imperative but also as indicating the very nature of things, embracing their truth as creatures of a God who is

---

1. Chiara Lubich, *Essential Writings*, p. 169.
2. The 20th edition in Italian containing original writings has been recently published (Chiara Lubich, *Meditazioni*, Rome 2020).

love. It expresses faith in the unity that holds together all of creation, faith in the unity that exists between heaven and earth.

Though Chiara clearly sees God and the world, heaven and earth, eternity and history, as distinct, she never sees them as separated. In this chapter, when we use the expression Paradise '49 to refer to her experience and her writings thereof, we do so always against the background of the great mystery of the Christian faith, the mystery of a God who has become human, who made himself "nothing" (an expression used in some of these texts) to give us his all and to gather us and all his creation to himself.

The salvific event of Christ has a definitive and ultimate value, but it becomes manifest in history as something that is limited and passing, and in so doing communicates to our limited and passing world a horizon of eternity. For this reason, we speak of the eschatological character of the Christ event and of the texts and experiences associated with it. Every true faith experience has this quality insofar as it "reads" human life from the horizon of God. In extraordinary experiences like those described in Paradise '49, by extending the limits of the spoken language, the eschatological character is even more explicitly evident, and in this way becomes a key to living in the world in all its concreteness.

When in this book the word "unity" is used, taking its cue from the text of Paradise '49, it will be used in this light. To speak of unity from the perspective "of Paradise," the perspective of Chiara Lubich's mystical experience, is not to speak of something beyond this world. Clearly, one needs an adequate hermeneutic so as not to approach mystical texts in a disingenuous way, and this requires a rigorous use of language associated with the various disciplines. However, to remain faithful to these texts also means to keep in mind the indissoluble bond between God and the world: to speak of one is to speak of the other and vice-versa.

The Call to Unity

> Unity!
> But who would dare speak of it?
> It's as ineffable as God!
> You feel it, you enjoy it… but it's ineffable!
> Everyone rejoices in its presence.
> Everyone suffers in its absence.
> It is peace, gladness, love, ardor, an atmosphere
> of heroism
> Of highest generosity.
> It's Jesus among us![3]

These words, from a letter written by Chiara Lubich in 1948 to a group of religious men, conveys the impact the charism had on those who adhered to it in the early years of the Movement. It was an experience of the living God in their midst that changed everything. Their conviction was that unity is God who transforms people, weaves them together, giving them the taste of heaven and allowing them to see the world in a new light.

> His light!…
> I want to talk to you and I don't know how.
> The voice of the heart is love
> The mind contemplates, filled with the beauty![4]

Unity is as ineffable as God. This exclamation expresses not only a theological truth, but the amazement of a faith that is experienced. The phrase "unity is as ineffable as God" also reminds us of how talk of unity within the horizon of the Trinity is always provisional and limited. If we move beyond religious language to an epistemological interpretation, the word "unity" would probably have a different sense for each field of knowledge and

---

3. Chiara Lubich, *Early Letters: At the Origins of a New Spirituality*, p. 103.
4. Ibid., p. 104.

for each sector of society. How then does one write a trans-disciplinary book around a word that has so many meanings, without running the risk of speaking each time of something different and of being confused in our language? "Who would dare speak of it?" applies also in this sense.

This book then is not proposing an inquiry into the meaning of the word "unity" in the various fields of thought, because probably in that case each would be saying something different. Rather, it is a reflection on those intuitions that Chiara initially intended when she wrote: "Unity is the synthesis of our spirituality."[5] What we are opening up is a description of and reflection on the lifestyle that is typical of members of the Focolare Movement that takes as its horizon Jesus' prayer in chapter 17 of John's Gospel: "... that all may be one; as you, Father, are in me and I in you, that they also may be in us."

The point of departure is life, experience. Various social realities and indeed academic reflections have emerged in various fields from this Movement defined by its spirituality of "unity." There should exist therefore a common denominator, a point of departure, a fixed point that allows all, even among those working in different fields, to be able to make their own the words of Chiara and say, "Unity is our vocation"[6]—even if perhaps they do not speak specifically of unity but express it in a language specific to their own discipline. What ties together persons from different social and cultural backgrounds sharing a common passion is a common "calling" notwithstanding a multiform context and different modes of expression.

What does this calling consist of? What type of life is born from a spirituality "of unity"? What are the specific traits through which one can know that a given experience is an authentic experience "of unity"? What does it mean to live unity in accordance with the charism of Chiara Lubich? Do

---

5. Chiara Lubich, *The Secret of Unity*, p. 20.
6. Ibid.

certain criteria exist for discernment? Are there visible signs that identify this expression of life and thought, as a life and thought rooted in the gift that God has granted to humanity through Chiara? How does one express unity both in thought and in action within the various fields of culture and science?

Certainly, a modest book like this one cannot answer all these questions. Its task is only to trace some lines of response. Beginning with the present chapter it wants to go to the root of this topic and offer a first reading of the text of Paradise '49 from the perspective of unity. In so doing, it will serve as the point of departure for other parts of the book that will seek to understand if and in what way the reading and the life of Paradise '49 offer criteria that can inspire and guide those who want to live their faith in depth, those who work in society and those who undertake research in specific disciplines.

The Book of Light: Unity and Jesus Forsaken

For what follows the text of Paradise '49 will be the principal reference. However, it is based on an important premise: Chiara Lubich did not acquire the charism of unity only in 1949 when a special mystical period began. Already from the outset of her journey, and no later than 1943 with the start of the Movement, she was guided by a light that attracted hundreds and later thousands of people, who gathered around the first focolare houses, and which found its expression in the cardinal points of a new spirituality that was already clearly emerging in those first years.

Each time that Chiara recounted the story of the beginning—what she called "the story of the Ideal"—she recalled that moment when together with her companions she read "by candlelight the testament of Jesus,"[7] that is, chapter 17 of the Gospel of John, which would become the magna carta of their life. It is sufficient to read some of the letters from the early times to recognize how the ideal and life of unity was making headway. Indeed, from these writings some important elements emerge:

– The horizon of unity is universal. For Chiara the prayer for unity, Jesus' last will and testament in chapter 17 of John's Gospel, could not but be universal. Taking a cue from something St. Catherine of Siena said, Chiara extended it even more:

> St. Catherine of Siena said it: "If you are what you should be, you'll put fire in all of Italy [the world!]. Don't be happy with small things, because he, the Lord God, wants great things!"… And we want all the peoples of the earth for our inheritance. He said it himself: "*Postula a me et dabo tibi*"… "Let's believe him in unity."[8]

– Unity is the divine presence between people; it is life in God because "Jesus is among us."[9] This presence is awesome and communicates joy: "Oh, unity, unity! What a divine beauty! Human words are not able to express it! It's: Jesus."[10]

– Unity is a work of God. But God works through men and women, and therefore "we offer him our existence," our nothingness so as to make space for all that God wants.

---

7. Ibid., p. 21.
8. Letter of 11 May 1948 to Fr. Bonaventura da Malé, OFM CAP. See *Early Letters*, pp. 109-110. The phrase in Latin refers to Ps 2:8: "Ask of me, and I will make the nations your heritage."
9. Letter of 29 April 1948 to a group of consecrated religious. See *Early Letters*, p. 103.
10. Letter of August 1947 to Fr. Raffaele Massimei, OFM CONV. See *Early Letters*, p. 83.

– Unity sheds light on human nature in general and on each person; it is a bond between people that makes them be what they are according to God's design: "In this unity willed by God, the two souls are fused into *one* and then blossom *equal but distinct*."[11]

– Unity is missionary fire, because the life of God which is tangible among human persons also attracts others: "any soul that meets *Jesus* (Jesus among us) will be inexorably immersed in his love."[12]

This strong conviction regarding the centrality of unity and the spreading of the life that it brought in the early years of the Movement cannot be understood without an intuition that goes back to the beginning of the Movement and has to do with the redemptive work of Christ, which for Chiara can be subsumed under the name "Jesus Forsaken." The tight bond between unity and Jesus Forsaken is expressed through an image that Chiara on various occasions used to describe the heart of the spirituality of the Focolare. In a letter of 30 March 1948, she uses the image of a coin with two sides:

> The book of light that the Lord is writing in my soul has two aspects: one, a page shining with mysterious love: unity. The other page, shining with mysterious pain: Jesus Forsaken. They are two sides of the same coin.[13]

In this image there are two fundamental intuitions. In the first place it is necessary to underline that unity and Jesus Forsaken are inseparable. This is a fundamental point and needs to be well understood. It is not a question of a journey and its end,

---

11. Letter of 11 May 1948 to Fr. Bonaventura da Malé, OFM CAP. See *Early Letters*, p. 108.

12. Letter of 27 December 1948 to Father Bonaventura, OFM CAP. See *Early Letters*, p. 136.

13. *Early Letters*, p. 93.

of a means (Jesus Forsaken) to an end (unity). Jesus Forsaken is called by Chiara "the key to unity," but not a key in the sense that once the door is unlocked it serves no more purpose. It is the key to understanding, in the sense that one does not understand unity if not as the key to God's love, a love that is expressed in a special way by the cry of Jesus on the cross: "My God, my God, why have you forsaken me?" Chiara was convinced that "Every light on unity stems from that cry."[14] It is the key in the sense of life: there's no life of unity unless that which is given by Jesus Forsaken to humanity. The life of unity is a sharing in him, with him. Jesus Forsaken is not "something else" with respect to unity. He is the other side of the coin, of the same coin that is love: the love which is Jesus, the expression of the love of the Father.[15] It is love that is contemporaneously both nothing (in the sense of a complete gift) and all. Life in God is therefore life in a "nothingness-all of love," as Chiara will call it in the text of Paradise '49. Unity is God, Jesus Forsaken is God.[16]

Another intuition contained in the image of the two-sided coin is tied to the fact that it has depth or density. To speak of density means to speak of matter, of time and space, in other words of all that is not (pure) spirit (and idea). Unity and Jesus Forsaken are not merely two abstract ideas, spiritual intuitions without flesh. They are real life with all that that implies. Chiara Lubich wrote that all the words of the Gospel are contained between the two sides of the coin,[17] that gospel that itself recounts and is made up of so many concrete stories of men and women, the gospel that generates new life, inspired by an infinity of new stories. Only within and through life do

---

14. Ibid.
15. In a letter dated July 1948 to all the members of the Movement, Chiara wrote: "Love and suffering are synonymous in the earthly life." See *Early Letters*, p. 115.
16. Ibid., p. 110.
17. Chiara Lubich, *Essential Writings*, p. 16.

we comprehend the true sense of these two sides of the coin and the relationship between them.

The two then are inseparable, and together they are a power of life and intellectual light. This latter aspect of light can be found repeated in many of Chiara's letters from 1943 to 1949. The charism that she received as a gift from God is a charism of light that helps all who allow themselves to be touched by it to understand their life and to discover the golden thread in all that surrounds them. "The book of light" is what Chiara called it when she used the image of the coin. A book of light that would later open up into a mystical experience of what is now called Paradise '49.

Turned toward the Father

Let our souls look only upon the Father.[18]

July 16, 1949 initiates an experience that is called Paradise '49. It begins with the so-called pact of unity between Chiara Lubich and Igino Giordani, which has been extensively analyzed in the first volume of studies by the Abba School published in Italian some years ago. It is significant that although only two people were involved initially, this pact had a much wider dimension, because Chiara rejected the idea of simply a two-person unity— it seemed to her to be reductive, given the great divine design entailed by the prayer of Jesus "that all may be one," taken from John's Gospel. Therefore, she proposed to Giordani (whom she referred to with the familiar name of Foco) that he leave it to Jesus to bring about whatever he wanted:

> And I added: "You know my life: I am nothing. I want to live, indeed, like Jesus Forsaken who annihilated

---

18. *P'49*, 402, August 1949.

himself completely. You too are nothing because you live in the same way. So then, we will go to church tomorrow and I will say to Jesus-Eucharist who will come into my heart, as into an empty chalice: 'On the nothingness of me please make unity with Jesus-Eucharist in Foco's heart. And, Jesus, bring about between us the bond which is known to you.'" Then I added: "And you, Foco, do the same."[19]

The words "On the nothingness of me…," proposed as a prayer, not only express the appropriate spiritual disposition of the believer who is conscious of the infinite God, but for Chiara, these words also carried the imprint of an experience from the first years of the Movement, which on the one hand was marked by many fruits and unexpected developments, but on the other also by accusations and difficulties, especially in 1948 when Chiara was on the verge of seeing everything collapse.[20] She was very aware that if the Movement were to remain and grow it would all be God's work. The nothingness of which Chiara speaks, as well as being desired and embraced in faith, is a lived existential emptiness. On this nothingness expressed in the pact with Foco, heaven opened up to her:

> I entered and went before the tabernacle. And there I was about to pray to Jesus-Eucharist and say to him: "Jesus." But I could not. That Jesus, who was in the tabernacle, was also here in me, was me too, was me, identified with him. Therefore I could not

---

19. *P'49*, 24-25.

20. In this context, Chiara's letter to Fr. Massimei of 15 June 1948 speaks of the "acute suffering" from continuing "to watch everything fall apart," of the destruction "after six years of building." At the same time she says that "Unity is not the focolares, … the approvals, or disapprovals. Unity is something beyond all these things. It's heavenly peace—it's complete joy—it's perfect light that illuminates the thickest darkness—it's pure and ardent love … it's: Jesus." See Chiara Lubich, *Early Letters*, p. 111.

call out to myself. And there I discovered coming spontaneously from my mouth the word: "Father." And in that moment I found myself within the bosom of the Father.[21]

In this rather concise description of the beginning of what was later to be called Paradise '49, two decisive points are highlighted with regard to unity:

– Unity is never something closed, it is never just unity of a group; rather it is always open to the horizon of "*ut omnes,*" in other words, that all be one.

– In the unity between two people there is always a third element, in which and from which one can speak of unity in the Christian sense of the term. In the account of the pact, it is the transition from Jesus-Eucharist to the Father.

"I found myself in the bosom of the Father," is how Chiara describes her first impressions, as if it were a change of place. However, what opened up for her on 16 July 1949 was an experience that did not distance her from the world in which she lived. Rather, the point was that she had the clear sense that her whole perspective had changed. It was like the experience of a person who has normally lived in a dark room and suddenly someone switches on the light: finally, one sees where they truly are. So in this "journey in paradise," as Chiara herself sometimes referred to it, she seemed to see all things, including the world and persons in their true reality, in other words, as they are "from God's" perspective.

God sees all of creation "from unity." Unity is the life of God himself. It is the design God has for humanity, embracing all and everyone. In the account of the prayer of Jesus in John 17, Jesus addresses his Father; he is completely one with him

---

21. *P'49*, 26.

and all is directed toward the Father to whom Jesus will return after his earthly life, opening the way for all of humanity.

Chiara, together with her companion focolarine, on numerous occasions had read this chapter of John's Gospel. Now, with the experience of paradise, the full depth and revolutionary understanding of the chapter came to light for them: Jesus, as he prays to the Father, includes and brings with him all his followers, all who believe in him. This indeed is the nucleus of what unity is for Chiara in this experience of Paradise '49. It is the experience of the human person with Jesus and in Jesus being directed toward the Father—toward that Father who, being love, brings his sons and daughters, all of humanity, to live the same love among them.

The so-called third narrative of the pact, written in August 1949 (and historically the first text to actually describe this initial moment) expresses all of this in a very precise manner. It is written not as a narrative but in the form of a meditation that reflects upon and penetrates the mystery. It expresses the wonder of both of them finding themselves in the Father, together with Jesus and in Jesus.

> We understood that being consummated in one and basing our life's journey on *unity,* we were Jesus who journeyed. He who is Way in us became Wayfarer. And we were no longer ourselves, but he in us: he the divine fire who consummated our two very different souls in a third soul: his own: all Fire. So we were One and Three. Jesus and Jesus in him; Jesus in me; Jesus among us. The place that received us, a ciborium with One Jesus or Three
> We were Jesus, and because we were Jesus, we were Mary.
> And the Jesus in me presented himself before the tabernacle to communicate, since he could not communicate with my brother, because my brother was me, was Jesus.

And the heart needs to communicate, just as it needs life.

With whom? How? Who remains for it beyond this? Is not everything done? And yet even being Jesus without being communion is a torment, death, hence not Jesus who is Life and Joy.

And from my lips came forth expressed by the Spirit a single word: *Father!*

And everything was accomplished. Nothing lacking at all.

I found my first love again: God-Love: Father.

And I saw the life of Jesus again all intent on a single "greater than I," the only one good: Father.

And I heard the answer to the Apostles again that praying is saying few words, hence: Our Father.

Hence Jesus loses himself in the Father and if he says to pray to him in his name, it is because he said: "Whoever sees me sees the Father."

We: sons, daughters in the Son in the Father.

And Jesus at our side looks and makes us look upon One Alone: the Father.

At our side and in us: for through his eyes we look upon the Father.

When night has fallen the world without sun is illuminated by the moon and the stars.

Likewise the souls, who did not find the Father while staying in Jesus, in the heaven of their soul have and look upon the Virgin and the saints.

But when the sun rises, the moon disappears, as do the stars, and, even if they are there, they are lost in the light of the sun: the light shed by the Sun is Jesus and the Sun is the Father.

Let our souls look only upon the Father.

In him they will find again Mary and the saints made God. Our mother and our brothers and sisters there Above want to be looked upon like this, for their Paradise is the Father.[22]

On re-reading this text after many years within the context of the Abba School, Chiara reaffirmed the importance and the novelty of the experience. Indeed, she had the following footnote added to the text:

> The discovery of the Father was a conversion for us. . . . religion is this: before all else to look to the Father; afterwards, in the Father, we find everything.[23]

In the Father we find everything. In the Father we find—as noted in the conclusion—Mary and the saints. In the Father we find all our other brothers and sisters, loved as we are. In the Father we find all of creation in its true order. In relation to the Father all takes its proper position. To speak of unity in the sense of Paradise '49 means to speak of how all things are ordered by the Father and toward the Father; it is to speak of human beings consciously deciding to lose and rediscover themselves in this divine order.

My True Self

No matter how much unity (in the sense of the charism of Chiara Lubich) is an experience of people linked together, the fact is that it cannot be understood or lived without the root of unity and the possibility of being in the "third," that is, without being in God-the-Father from whom all goes forth and returns, and being in God-the-Son who is the divine presence in the midst of human reality. The reference to the "third" allows us

---

22. *P'49*, 384-403, August 1949.
23. *P'49*, 384, note 326.

to transcend the partial bonds and limitations that are present in a group of people. Unity that is rooted in God is not based on common objectives (even though they might be holy), on similar opinions, on linguistic or cultural ties, on membership of a particular group or movement. All of this could be useful, but this is still not unity. It would exclude all those who are not similar, and it would exclude a lot of our own self. Unity is something more; it includes our whole being, not simply what we have in common but also what distinguishes us like our culture, language, and character, and our individuality.

Unity is expressed as an experience of mutual love and for this reason it attracts and spreads. However, it is not simply the fruit of this love: if unity depended on the degree of sanctity necessary to have true and constant love toward our neighbor it would be a utopia or would remain constrained by the frailty of mere human love. It would not be the unity in accordance with Chiara's charism embracing the horizon "That all may be one" (*ut omnes*), the horizon of that "third" that surpasses and embraces all individual aspects. Only by referring to the "third" is it possible to maintain unity and diversity at the same time. To look toward the Father means to recognize and appreciate the richness of pluriformity. Each one of us in his or her uniqueness is linked to the Father. The Father is the root and within the root everyone is to be found.

Various texts of Paradise '49 express this. There is a very eloquent piece from 23 July 1949 worth noting:

> The Kingdom of Heaven is in the bosom of the Father. The Father has an expression of himself outside himself, made as it were of diverging rays, and an expression within himself, made of rays that converge in the center, in a point that is Love: God in the infinitely small: the "Nothing-All" of Love! The Word.

> The diverging rays are Jesus. By means of Jesus the
> Father reaches all his children outside himself in
> whatever point they are to be found.
> As bit by bit these come closer to God, walking
> along the will of God (being Jesus), they come closer
> to one another.
> The converging rays in the heart of the Sun which is
> the Father, are Word of God, are Word converging
> in the Word...
> The Father says: "love" in infinite tones and begets
> the Word, who is love, within himself, the Son,
> and the Son being the Son, echo of the Father, says
> "Love" and returns to the Father![24]

The image of the sun with its rays that reach the world is a
well-known analogy within religious thought. However, Chiara
speaks not only of diverging rays but also of converging ones
within God, which come together in the infinitely small, concentrated in a point, in whose image Chiara sees "the Word"—"a
'Nothing-All' of Love ."

Both the diverging rays and the rays converging in the
center are expressions of the one God, who expresses himself
both outside and inside himself. And both being expressions
of God (although within different modalities and different
"spaces"), both types of rays are equally expressions of unity. The
divergence (within the infinite richness of creation) is always
an expression of the Father, of the one God, of unity. Equally
notable is the description of God's interior. The passage again
speaks of a pluriformity of rays, no less a pluriformity than that
of the external rays: the Father "pronounces 'love' in infinite
tones." These infinite tones mean that God's interior is not to
be thought of as a oneness in which all difference has vanished;
rather God is truly one *being* an infinite multiplicity.

---

24. *P'49*, 97-101, 23 July 1949.

There is therefore a unity "outside" (in the divergence) and a multiplicity "inside" (within the convergence) and vice versa. Unity and multiplicity are in no way opposites but exist only together—because one cannot think of the Father if not as infinite richness. A text from 25 August 1949 says this in a concise way: "In Paradise the deeper one enters, the more Unity and Distinction are accentuated."[25]

It is within this vision from Paradise '49 that Chiara sees and describes the human person. Each one of us, she notes, is a word pronounced by the Father from eternity. In this unique Word of the Father (who is the Son, the *Verbum*) there is an infinity of words, each one different from the other. My true being, my uniqueness, is anchored in heaven because God loves and creates each person in a different, unique and unrepeatable way. A short text from 25 July 1949 expresses it this way:

> I (the idea of me) is "ab aeterno" [from all eternity] in the Mind of God, in the Word; therefore, "ab aeterno" I am loved by the Father and "ab aeterno" I hold the place the Father has assigned me. And it is there Above, that is, my true "I": Christ in me. There Above I am that Word of God which "ab aeterno" God has uttered.
> And I am God. Therefore, even were I not to be saved, God "ab aeterno" and for all eternity would see me and delight in me, just as I ought to have been.[26]

My true self is that which is written in heaven. My true self is Christ in me. However, this affirmation is to be understood in a double sense. It does not mean that my true self is identical to the person beside me, in the sense that both of us lose ourselves in an indistinct collective identity, but rather precisely because

---

25. *P'49*, 482, 25 August 1949.
26. *P'49*, 244, 25 July 1949.

it is anchored in Christ, each one's unique personal identity is different from every other person. Nor does it mean—and this would be another possible misunderstanding—that my identity, unique and personal, is a fixed entity as if it were almost pre-established by God. Rather because we are loved by God, this "I" is left free to carry out its journey within human history through each one's personal choices, having the possibility, through our lives, to put "flesh" on that word which is within our inner depth. To the extent that it is such, to the extent that there is a unique and free "I," it can be in a profound and true communion with other persons.

In the footnote to this verse, Chiara deepens this intuition:

> Our personality therefore is the Christ in us. We, losing "our" personality, take on Christ's, which is much stronger, much more distinct. But we must have the courage to lose "our" personality, while in the world people are intent upon saving it. In this, Jesus Forsaken is truly the master. With him we too can reach the point of saying, "It is no longer I who live, but it is Christ who lives in me" (Gal 2:20).[27]

To be truly ourselves, we have to orient ourselves to that true "I" that is written in heaven, that has existed from all eternity in the Father. In the world, however, there are many other images and idols that say to us: it has to be like this or like that, one has to follow this or that tendency. The world, on the one hand, tends to assimilate us to each other and cheats us by suggesting that this is our true identity; on the other hand, it also asks us to affirm ourselves as an "I" closed within itself. Being aware of this double tendency, Chiara invites us to "lose our personality," in the sense of a mere superficial image of who we are. To be

---

27. *P'49*, 244, note 229.

ourselves, each one of us has to always return again to that true "I" that is Christ in us.

Within this anthropological framework of unity and plurality, of losing and being, the following short key phrase needs to be highlighted: "In this, Jesus Forsaken is truly the master." Chiara, in other words, necessarily reaches the point of that side of the coin without which unity would not exist. It is a profoundly personal act, specific for the life of the charism of unity. To be one among us—she says—it is necessary that each one be his or herself, meaning that true self that reflects the word said by God when he thought of us. Each of us is this "I" only by being "in God"; and to enter into God in this way means being all that is indicated and expressed by the name "Jesus Forsaken": "You are God, you are my God, *our* God of infinite love."[28] Our God—affirms Chiara—is Jesus Forsaken.

Jesus Forsaken: the Nothing-all of Love

The last phrase of the preceding paragraph has two meanings. To say our God is Jesus Forsaken is both an affirmation of *who God is in himself* and of *who God is for us* or, in other words, it is an affirmation of how we have access to him. Taken together they affirm what love is for us. Both meanings are tied together in an essential way. As Christian theology teaches us, of *God in himself* we know nothing except for that which has been revealed to humanity insofar as he is, also, *God for us.* There isn't a God who is hidden and different from that of revelation. Nevertheless, it is correct to speak separately of both perspectives in order to maintain the difference between God and the world, which should not be mixed. When Chiara Lubich uses

---

28. *P'49*, 1316, summer of 1950.

the name of Jesus Forsaken not only to indicate the possibility of an encounter between God and the world and creation's way back to God, but also to express something about God in himself, she is being faithful to the Christian tradition.

To say something about God in himself, it is useful to cite a short text from 8 December 1949 with its accompanying footnote, which will help us draw closer to the world of Paradise '49 and the mystery of God's unity.

> Jesus Forsaken is a miracle of nulliufying that which is. A miracle comprehensible only to one who knows Love and knows that in Love *all* and *nothing* coincide.
>
> If we consider the Word in the Father, we think of the Word as nothing (a nothingness of love) to be able to think of God-one.
>
> If we consider the Father in the Word, we think of the Father as nothing (a nothingness of Love).
>
> Jesus Forsaken clothed the All with Nothingness to nullify Nothingness and give divine consistency to all that passes: "All is vanity of vanities" (Eccl 1:2).[29]

In these few lines we find the most important of Christian theological questions: How does one conceive of a God who is both one and three? What is love? How are we to think of the connection between God and the world, as a connection that leads us from the world (meaning from creation, from the not divine) to God?

Chiara Lubich refers to the notion of being "nothing." It is a key word that recurs often in the text of Paradise '49, and as such has to be understood well. Since it refers here to God, it is evident that it is a "nothing" that is eminently positive: "in God, in love, *all* and *nothing* coincide." It is in this light that we

---

29. *P'49*, 1024-1027, 8 December 1949.

also need to understand those sections that speak of "nothing" in reference to human life. Being "nothing" or "nothingness" is always an open door, as it was in the pact, when the "nothingness" of Chiara and Foco opened heaven to them. It is the space through which the divine enters the human person.

Indeed, upon rereading the above cited piece during a meeting of the Abba School, Chiara was aware of its significance and commented on it with a long footnote which is here quoted in part:

> What I write here about the Word's being nothing in the Father and the Father's being nothing in the Word is important for comprehending God-One. The Three, in the Trinity, are One by mutual indwelling. But to be One it is necessary that each of the Three be truly nothing, a great nothing, a divine nothing, with regard to their being one. We ought to penetrate this being nothing of theirs, this total inexistence of theirs. Without doubt it remains a mystery how in the Trinity the Word is nothing and at the same time is the Son, and likewise for the Father and the Spirit. Certainly God, being love, is able to make himself nothing. Therefore, it is Jesus Forsaken, love totally opened out, who in some way can shed light on this mystery for us. I think it is as if each of the divine Persons, in making themselves nothing, were clothing themselves in Jesus Forsaken, because Jesus Forsaken is God clothed in nothingness, complete nothingness. It is he therefore who for us can open up God-one, even if immediately afterwards everything again seems wrapped in mystery.[30]

---

30. *P'49*, 1027, note 777.

In this footnote Chiara uses the word "mystery" more than once. She is aware that here our knowledge and our discourses come up against a limit. However, mystery does not mean that we have to be silent but rather that our reflection on the subject will never be sufficient. We need to live, reflect, recount and communicate.

When Chiara speaks of Jesus Forsaken, certainly she is thinking of the paschal event that took place within human history. But for her, as she understood it in the experience of Paradise '49, this historical event expressed the mystery of God's existence, the mystery of unity.

A Passion for the World

Unity, therefore, has its roots and its origin in God. That which can be said of the mystery of unity in God can also be applied to the possibility of unity among human persons. It is particularly valid for those people who live a spirituality of unity, who live within a Movement that sees itself called to be an instrument of unity in the world. This too—and it could not be otherwise—has to be understood as beginning with and within Jesus Forsaken, because, "In him is the whole of paradise with the Trinity and the whole of earth with humanity," and "I will go through the world seeking him in every instant of my life," as pronounced in one of the famous pages of Chiara Lubich's writings.[31] This seeking means to be one of his followers, it means to make his passion our own and in so doing go beyond all barriers and seek that which is lost, human beings and also all of creation:

---

31. From the writing: "I Have Only One Spouse on Earth," in Chiara Lubich, *Essential Writings*, p. 95.

Lord, give me all who are lonely… I have felt in my heart the passion that fills your heart for all of the forsakenness in which the whole world is drifting. I love every being that is sick and alone. Even the suffering of plants causes me pain… even the animals that are alone.

Who consoles their weeping?

Who mourns their slow death?

Who presses to their own heart, the heart in despair? My God, let me be in this world the tangible sacrament of your love, of your being love; let me be your arms that press to themselves and consume in love all the loneliness of the world.[32]

When this "consuming in love" becomes reciprocal between two persons, the presence of the risen Jesus can become manifest in them and so his living presence can be experienced in their midst, thereby renewing society. The text *The Resurrection of Rome*, although not the only one, is in this sense a most eloquent text on this theme.[33]

Jesus Forsaken is the form of love, however, not only when one strives to take on the passion of this troubled world. He also has to be the form of love present in each encounter among people in the sense of having an attitude of listening profoundly and respecting the true being of each one, the true being that can be a gift for us. We read this in a short text:

To take into self the All it is necessary to be nothingness like Jesus Forsaken. And on nothingness everyone can write… It is necessary to put ourselves

---

32. Ibid., p. 81.

33. Ibid., p. 173. The Abba School dedicated one of its publications in Italian to this topic. See Hubertus Blaumeiser and Anna Maria Rossi (eds.), *Risurrezione di Roma. Dialoghi interdisciplinari su città, persona e relazioni a partire da un testo di Chiara Lubich*, Rome 2017.

> before everyone in an attitude of learning, for we really have something to learn. And only nothingness gathers all into itself and clasps to itself each thing in unity: it is necessary to be nothing (Jesus Forsaken) before each brother or sister in order to clasp *Jesus* to ourselves in them.[34]

If it is true that a "nothingness-all" of love is, for whoever follows the charism of Chiara Lubich, a way to encounter each and every person, this attitude is also valid for the relationships among those who live the spirituality of unity, and so for the relationships within the Movement. In the second part of the text of Paradise '49 there are intuitions and indicators that bear witness to this with regard to life within Focolare communities and the newly born Movement. We will return to this topic in the second part of the book. Here it is sufficient just to mention it.

In Paradise '49 when referring to our relationship with God or to relationships among people, certain expressions like "to lose," "to renounce," "to annihilate," "to cancel out" occur often. These expressions can be understood in a correct way in the light of all that has been said within this chapter. The coin has two sides, unity and Jesus Forsaken, that are inseparable in every act and every moment of life but especially when we encounter one another:

> … when a brother or sister speaks, we have to negate everything (even divine inspirations) so as to enter into our brother or sister perfectly, having made ourselves *nothing* and therefore simple. Only simplicity enters everywhere. And this means being *one*. And here is seen how being one is being Jesus Forsaken.[35]

---

34. *P'49*, 539-540, 28 August 1949.
35. *P'49*, 1133, 3 April 1950.

"Being one is being Jesus Forsaken." These words are significant. They issue a strong challenge, because each step "through nothingness" reverberates on an existential level, on the level of feelings. A life of unity among human beings does not come about without encountering the inevitable and mysterious reality of suffering. But we can understand it if we keep in mind what has been said previously about the human person: unity as being in the Father does not cancel out our personhood but anchors it in eternity where unity and multiplicity are not two opposites, but presuppose each other. The being nothing, of which we are here speaking, is a transition and is not an indistinct nothingness, it is not a nothingness without a face, it is not anonymous; it is not an emptiness. It is "a willed nothingness,"[36] it is my nothingness of love: it is my irreplaceable "I" who, with my unique personality, give of myself and receive myself back again, transformed and filled with the life of God.

A final point. The life of unity is not a life outside of the real world. Nothingness is not poetry; it is not the nothingness of a silent meditation somewhere outside the din of the world. The nothingness that God lived, coming on earth in Jesus in order to recompose unity, is the nothingness of the cross: that nothingness in which he took upon himself all the evil of this world. The nothingness of love of which Chiara Lubich speaks in *Paradise '49* is *this* nothingness of Jesus. It means to be in the midst of the world, seeking out, with and within Jesus "the suffering that grazes me in the present,"[37] so as to allow Jesus the possibility of transforming it, knowing that it is not we who build unity, but rather discover it—and in this way make it emerge—as the truth hidden beneath all beings created and loved by God.

---

36. In Italian it is written as "nulla voluto." Refers to *P'49*, 19 April 1950.
37. *P'49*, 650, 20 September 1949.

Part Two
Further Insights

3.– Unity and Diversity.
The Experience of the Soul

by Lucia Abignente, Stefan Tobler and Hubertus Blaumeiser

In Paradise, the deeper one enters, the more
Unity and Distinction are accentuated.[1]

This sentence from the Paradise '49 text is taken from a note
dated 25 August 1949, at a time when the succession of intuitions, of "intellectual visions"[2] as Chiara herself puts it, about
life in God was particularly intense. It's a sentence that touches
on a fundamental anthropological question, with implications
for personal relationships and for social and political life too.

Unity and distinction, unity and difference are not mu-
tually exclusive, but can—according to the affirmation just
quoted—go hand in hand and even strengthen each other. In
what sense, then, does unity between persons—the theme of
this book—include and presuppose individuality? And in what
sense can one's own individuality be developed in such a way as
to facilitate relationships that bring people together, and indeed
"fuse them together"—as Chiara sometimes says—in unity?

In the following pages we will explore some intuitions
regarding the theme of unity. We will draw on various texts
from Paradise '49, taking into account the context in which they
arose during the summer of '49 and the months that followed.
Chiara felt that she and the first group of focolarini, with whom

---

1. *P'49*, 482, 25 August 1949.
2. Chiara uses the term "intellectual visions" in a passage of September 1950
(*P'49*, 1534) and also uses it in footnotes to the text that she put together in
the context of the Abba School's work on the text.

she shared the experience of those months, were immersed in a light that was new and different each day.

The variety of this light, an expression of God who says "love" in "infinite tones,"[3] left no doubt: unity carries within itself a great wealth of expressions.

This idea runs through the whole experience of Paradise '49 and is expressed in particular in what Chiara called the "Soul," the name given to the group that lived the extraordinary experience of unity and plurality during those months, a profound communion that reflected the uniqueness of each person. To explain better what this means, a premise is necessary. When speaking of the experience of the "Soul," something applies which is true of the whole of Chiara's charism. It did not begin suddenly in the summer of 1949, but had its roots and origin in the manner in which the experience of the Movement began in 1943. It is therefore important to take a look at that initial period.

In the Early Years of the Movement

It is well known that the dramatic growth during the difficult years of the Second World War in Trent of the group that became the Focolare Movement had its roots in the Gospel, and in a communitarian reality where the Word was listened to and put into practice. The fullest expression of this was found to be the prayer of Jesus, "That they may all be one" (Jn 17: 21) as the foundation and purpose of life. From a new understanding of these words and the commitment to make them come alive, a clear vision of unity already began to emerge in those early years. This can be seen, for example, in a writing of Chiara's from December 1946 which, among those that have

---

3. *P'49*, 101; see the expression in its context, p. 45.

been conserved, is the first to be entirely devoted to this subject. Among other things, we read:

> The soul must always direct its gaze above all else to the one Father of so many children. Then look upon all creatures as children of the one Father. Always transcend with thought and affection every limit set by human life and strive constantly and by habit for universal brotherhood in the one Father: God.[4]

Having emerged in the school of the Word of God, this vision impacted on the group's journey which in those years was rapidly experiencing a vast broadening of horizons. It gave rise to a belief soon becoming a certainty that, founded on the "one Father of so many children," they would reach the whole of Trent, Italy and the world. At the same time, this vision was enhanced further by an idea that is both simple and demanding—our neighbor "is the brother/sister who passes by us in the present moment of our lives."[5] This vision provided depth, continuity, and meaning as they strove to welcome and love everyone. The various attributes so often used to qualify people therefore proved to be secondary for them in the face of the fact that *every* neighbor is a son, a daughter of the Father to be served with love, in the certainty of serving God in him/her.[6]

For some time the gospel statement of Matthew 25:40 had placed in Chiara's heart a certainty of the presence of Jesus in every person: "Believe it: God is in you!" she wrote as early as 1943 in a circular letter.[7] While this awareness prompted the whole group to take on a demanding commitment to love everyone, even the most abandoned or rejected by society, it also "simplified" their outlook. This can be seen, for example, in the

---

4. Chiara Lubich, "L'Unità," in *Nuova Umanità* 29 (2007) 174, pp. 605-606.
5. Ibid., p. 607.
6. Ibid., p. 608.
7. Chiara Lubich, *Early Letters: At the Origins of a New Spirituality*, p. 2.

already mentioned writing on unity from 1946 where, by way of notes for a meditation talk she was to give, Chiara comments:

> The simple eye = seeing only one Father (= a single gaze) serving God alone in our neighbor. Having one brother: Jesus.
>
> The simple eye sees everyone as a "growing Christ." It places itself at the service of all these "other" Christs, in such a way that he comes to be and grows in them. It sees in each person a Christ who is born, a Christ who must grow and live, doing good—as a newborn child of God—and must die and rise in order to be glorified. "*Et ego claritatem, quam dedisti mihi, dedi eis, ut sint unum, sicut et nos unum sumus.*"[8]

Though the life that those young women were the first to embrace was undoubtedly a stimulating one, it was also a demanding commitment. If it was God who had "called them into one," this did not negate the variety among them. By way of example we could look at the first three companions who followed Chiara along the way of the focolare, her closest collaborators in the years leading up to 1949: Natalia Dallapiccola, considered her "first companion," Graziella de Luca, and Giosi Guella. Natalia's roots as well as her patient and sensitive nature were clearly seen in her almost angelic appearance, with her blonde curly hair and her smiling face full of wonder. She had a love for nature and for music, a love already evident during her peaceful childhood in a traditionally Christian family. At the same time we see in her experience the joy of having found again at the age of eighteen when she met Chiara the light and the purpose of life, after having experienced, after the premature

---

8. Chiara Lubich, "L'Unità," p. 608. The text finishes with John 17:22: *I have given them the glory that you gave me, that they may be one as we are one.*

death of her father, a "deep darkness," and the "conviction that love does not exist on earth."[9]

With her enviable beauty and spirit of initiative, Graziella's interests were quite different. She loved poetry and dancing, cinema and the theater. She was a successful basketball player, was offered a leading role in a film but also had the courage to withdraw from that environment when it conflicted with her idea of art. Whatever she wanted she achieved "without difficulty, and so it wasn't long before I became quite bored."[10]

With a "polite hostility" toward anything to do with the "sacristy," as she herself admitted,[11] she turned up at the Massaia Hall, where the Franciscan Third Order met, in an extravagant outfit. There was no way she could pass unobserved! Natalia prayed for her throughout the whole meeting, something which proved decisive for Graziella's life.

Giosi was different again. Coming from a tiny village of 450 inhabitants, from an early age she had known the sacrifice of work in the fields. After elementary school she had managed to go on and complete five years of secondary education, something not to be taken for granted at that time. To do this she had to walk eight kilometers every day, hail, rain or snow.

"We were the opposite of one another," admitted Graziella frankly. "I liked art and she liked doing accounts."[12]

Giosi's practical nature, her aptitude for mathematics and the sciences, saw her quickly assume a role of service to the whole community, attending to the daily needs of each person, whether it was to do with their food, clothing, health, or studies. She encouraged the creation of a wider communion of goods to meet the needs of destitute families.

9. Franca Zambonini, *Chiara Lubich, A Life for Unity*, London 1992, p. 156.

10. Ibid., p. 152.

11. Ibid.

12. From unpublished notes by Graziella De Luca, 21 May 2009.

Besides these three, the first group of companions in Trent was made up of other young women, very different in background and temperament. Some young men joined them: Marco Tecilla, a worker, Aldo Stedile, a painter, then other talented professionals followed, from Rome, Parma, Milan… Then, in 1948 the group received a very special gift in the form of the presence of Igino Giordani, a well-known writer and lay person admired for his wisdom and coherence. He was older than they, and had four children. At his first meeting with Chiara Lubich he recognized in her someone "inspired by the Holy Spirit"[13] and with enthusiasm made her ideal his own, soon acquiring the nickname "Foco." A wider community developed around them, extending to other cities, a community made up of people from all walks of life, vocations, and age groups.

This was a "polyphonic" choir, not called to a unity that annihilated the personality of each but rather, through the unreserved gift of self, which is the logic of divine life, each one "accepted the risk" of "losing" their life. It was a question of going beyond difficulties and continuously making new beginnings, as we can see from a letter Chiara wrote in 1947, while they were living the Word of Life, "Whoever remains in me and I in him, will bear much fruit" (Jn 15: 5).

This letter was written in reply to "Lucia," Raffaella Pisetta, a Franciscan tertiary, who had given Chiara hospitality in a small apartment in Piazza Cappuccini, which would later become the first focolare house. From the expressions used in the letter it can be seen that different views or feelings were not suppressed, and there was an effort to listen to others. Chiara writes:

> I know that Jesus *sees* and *knows* everything and that is why I have written to tell you that before passing judgment on the fact that I feel you are no longer

---

13. Igino Giordani, *Diary of Fire*, London 1981.

close to us, I wanted to hear what you have to say. I'm now convinced of this:

In practice, we are *one* and will always be one. The devil, however, is intent on breaking our unity a bit. In the meantime, we suffer, and if we love Jesus we can see in all of this a purification and thank the Lord for it.

Unity then, is just how you understand it. In order to not break unity, what is necessary from both sides is compassion, tolerance, love and understanding, allowing Jesus to be at his ease in our midst, united in his name.[14]

Chiara thus encourages her friend, "love, forgive everyone always, forget everything, and in the name of Mary *begin again* with your whole heart, with more light, with more experience, with more strength."[15]

Chiara's writings during those years speak of a constant and insistent recall to fraternal unity between people who are quite different from one another, and to how this unity can be maintained, reinforced, and deepened. Of fundamental importance for this is the life of the Gospel, sustained by the practice of exploring from time to time the Word of Life, one sentence taken each month from scripture to be lived throughout the month. "When are two souls consummated in one?" Chiara asks herself when writing to a religious in 1948. She replies, "When they are 'alive,' when they have been 'stripped' of their human side, their personality, and through the Word of Life lived, incarnated, they become 'living words.' Two *living words*

---

14. This letter is from Chiara Lubich to Raffaella Pisetta, 1 December 1947. The letter was published in part in *Vita Trentina* (special edition 23 December 2019, p.15), and the complete text was kindly given to us by a relative, Luisa Martinelli, to whom we are truly grateful.

15. Ibid.

can be consummated in one. If one of them is not *alive*, the other cannot be united to it."[16]

There are many examples that can clarify what she means by being "stripped" of the human side, one's personality. One such comes from 1948, not long before the summer of '49. Having moved to Rome, Chiara suddenly found herself in a comfortable environment, quite different from the one she had left in Trent. Seeing others with a "simple eye" was her continual effort in life. In one of the first days of her stay with the well-off Alvino family, she unhesitatingly wrote to the lady of the house asking forgiveness for a moment's lack of charity. We do not know the circumstances, but we can surmise that it was probably a judgment she had expressed, which served as an alarm bell to start again, seeing everything in God. Chiara wrote, "It seemed that Jesus was saying to me, 'Yes, you can criticize the rich in general, those who are attached to the things of this world... but you cannot touch personally my creatures who I love infinitely, and for whom I have given my blood!' And I recognized my mistake. Charity covers everything and I had done the opposite!"[17]

She felt the inner need to start again to love, and much more than previously. She added, "I take back absolutely every judgment made, even if this seems like a lack of character. My character is Jesus, and I must obey him who lives deep in my heart." It was a firm attitude, therefore, that revealed great interior strength.

There are other stories from the years before '49, in particular the period 1947-48, that make the efforts of these young women to build unity more "credible." They were moments in

---

16. Letter from Chiara Lubich to Raffaele Massimei OFM CONV, 23 October 1948, published with small variations in Chiara Lubich, *Early Letters*, pp. 129-131. The text used here is from the Chiara Lubich Archive (ACL), 120-00 01 05. The ACL is part of the General Archives of the Focolare Movement (AGMF) at Rocca di Papa (Rome).
17. Letter from Chiara Lubich to Elena Alvino, 18 December 1948.

which, amid the joy of the growth of the group, was added the pain of reservations or criticisms which came from outside, or as happened in 1948, from people very close to them. At those times, the steps that laid the foundation for their relationships helped them to hold firm and indeed to increase their resolve. Among these are three in particular: a) the pact of being ready to give one's life for the other, a spontaneous consequence of the new commandment of Jesus and the following statement, "No one has a greater love than this, to give his life for his friends (Jn 15:13); b) the so called "pact of mercy," the commitment to see one another anew each day, going beyond any perceived defects; and c) finally, the reconciliation before presenting oneself at the altar (Mt 5:23-24).

What we discover in those far from simple circumstances (paradoxically, one might say) is the reciprocal nature of giving that emerges in the Paradise of '49 as the law of nature and therefore of human nature.[18]

As a further example, we can refer to an episode from February 1949. Chiara wrote to Archbishop Carlo di Ferrari of Trent, seeking his agreement to meet with a young woman with whom she had been in very close contact but who later made accusations against her. "I know that she receives communion each day," she wrote, "just like I do. How can we not be united?" She explains:

> ... a strong sense of gratitude binds me to her, *more than to anyone*. I am grateful that she has been an instrument of God for my purification, and for having caused me to love my crucified spouse, abandoned by everyone, with my whole heart!

---

18. Chiara wrote on 2 September 1949: *I felt that I have been created as a gift for the one next to me and the one next to me has been created by God as a gift for me. As the Father in the Trinity is all for the Son and the Son is all for the Father. On earth all is in relationship of love with all: each thing with each thing. It is necessary to be Love to find the thread of gold among beings. (P'49, 548-549)*

> If she only knew how strong my desire is to draw
> close to her like a sister, not to convert her to unity,
> nor to be converted to her ideas, but simply to say
> with my visit that I still love her, more than before,
> and am ready to give my life for her.[19]

We see here a coherence, a logic that follows from what Chiara wrote in July 1949, "When any one of these souls of the pact shall make Jesus suffer, and in my own soul I feel this gash, I shall have to heal that soul, healing the gash in myself!"[20]

Circumstances that appeared "negative" prepared her to accept the gift that came from the pact with Foco in the Eucharist "on the nothingness of ourselves," which means "on our mutual love," because "living him" is "living the nothingness of ourselves in order to be all for God and for the others."[21]

The Experience of the Soul in Paradise '49

A feature of Chiara's mystical experience in the summer of '49 is the fact that from the start she shared and lived everything with Igino Giordani and the group that had grown up around her.

In Paradise she saw herself not alone, but as part of a group which she called "Soul." In a text from 1986, where she relates the first moments of her experience that summer, Chiara refers to aspects of life to be found in the expression "Soul." After telling about the moment of the pact with Igino Giordani[22] and the entry into the Father, she continues,

---

19. Letter from Chiara Lubich to Archbishop Carlo de Ferrari, in ACL, 140-01 01-01 02.
20. *P'49*, 270, 26 July 1949.
21. *P'49*, 11, note 17.
22. The pact of unity is referred to in the previous chapter, see above, pp. 44 to 49.

Foco, meanwhile, had come out of the friary and I invited him to sit with me on a bench next to a stream. And I said to him: "Do you know where we are?" And I explained to him what had happened to me. Then I went home where I met the focolarine, who I loved so much, and I felt urged to bring them up to date on everything. I then invited them to come with us to church the next day and to ask Jesus, who entered their hearts, to make the same pact with Jesus who entered ours. And they did so. After that I had the impression of seeing in the Bosom of the Father a small company: it was us. I communicated this to the focolarine who made such a great unity with me that they too had the impression of seeing each thing.

In the meantime, we did not cease *living*, living with intensity, amid our tasks about the house, the reality that we were, living the Word of Life.

Every morning we received Communion, letting Jesus bring about what he desired, while in the evening at six o'clock in church, before the altar of Our Lady, which was to the right of the main altar, we meditated in a rather original fashion. Thinking that Jesus wanted to communicate something of what he had brought about by the new Communion we had received, I invited the focolarine and myself not to think of anything, to nullify every thought so that he could enlighten us.

In the fire of the Trinity we had, in fact, been so fused into one that I called our company "Soul." We were the Soul. Now the Lord, if he wished, could enlighten this Soul (through me because I was like its center) about the new realities and so it seemed necessary for us to have the deepest inner silence. Then I communicated what I had understood to Foco and the focolarine. Our communions, therefore, were three: with Jesus-Eucharist, with his Word, and among us.[23]

In this passage many points refer specifically to that moment in time, but what is outlined also indicates characteristics of the life of unity that were typical of the spirituality of the Movement:

– *The basis is the pact of unity.* Chiara invited the focolarine to make the same pact with her that she had made the previous day with Igino Giordani, in which she placed herself in front of Jesus in the Eucharist asking him to bring about "on the nothingness of myself," hers and Foco's, the bond that only God could create. Making the pact means putting one's life in the hands of Another, allowing oneself to be led where he wants, asking Jesus himself to live his life in each one. This pact is renewed each day at the celebration of the Eucharist.

– *Love as a welcoming.* In the context of the experience that Chiara lived with her first companions "becoming nothing" is not a negative term. Rather, it describes the awareness of their own condition—welcomed in love—as creatures in front of the creator. To offer one's own nothingness in order for him to live in them meant living a mutual welcoming of love, in order for God to show himself. The focolarine, writes Chiara, "made such a great unity with me that they too had the impression of seeing everything."

– *Spiritual communion of goods.* Right from the start, Chiara shared everything. She couldn't but communicate because she was urged from within to do so, starting with Foco and the focolarine, and to widen the circle more and more. It is a mark of love to want to share with others what has been received. Chiara repeats this several times in the pages of Paradise '49. She writes that her companions have the "right" to share in

---

23. *P'49*, 32-37.

everything, "being my very own Soul,"[24] and "no sooner were they [the mysteries of light] communicated to the rest of the Soul than we perceived them to be shared."[25] Unity means circulating goods among everyone with a view to forming one single body, the "body of Christ," as it was called right from the first moments of the early Christian community.

– *Being Church*. The last paragraph of the text above, which speaks of three "communions" leads to the heart of the Church as a body of persons who live in communion with Jesus. The intense daily life of the Word and the Eucharist—pillars of the Church—accompany and nourish the "journey in paradise." Alongside these is a third communion, the communion "among us," that is, the presence of Jesus in the midst of his followers in accordance with his promise "Where two or three…" (Mt 18: 20). It is the communion with God expressed in concrete love, lived through "our household chores," Chiara writes, meaning in daily life, in the midst of the world.

In order to complete and further explore these points, highlighted in the above account of Paradise '49 that was written up in 1986, it is useful to look at another text closer in time to the events themselves. In December 1949, Chiara felt she had to describe some of the key moments of the first days of the mystical experience of that summer. She described in a much shortened form the pact, the entry into the bosom of the Father, and the Soul. She begins,

> But when two of us, knowing ourselves to be noth-
> ing, prompted Jesus-Eucharist to seal a pact of *unity*
> upon our two souls, I became aware that I was Jesus.
> I felt the impossibility of communicating with Jesus
> in the tabernacle. I experienced the elation of being
> at the peak of the pyramid of all creation, as on the

---

24. *P'49*, 278, 26 July 1949.
25. *P'49*, 340, 28 July 1949.

> point of a pin; at the point where the two rays meet, where the two who are God (so to speak) seal a pact of unity, becoming trinitized where, having been made Son in the Son, it is impossible to communicate with anyone except the *Father,* just as the Son communicates with the Father alone.[26]

The whole experience of paradise that summer is permeated by the awareness of who the human person is in front of God. "Knowing ourselves to be nothing," writes Chiara. She's not referring here to some classical effort of asceticism, or a moral judgment, but simply to a statement of a fact seen in the light of God's truth. On this basis God can work. At that special moment of grace, Chiara becomes aware that her whole being has been transported elsewhere—to use a spatial image—and transformed. She goes on:

> It is the point where the created dies into the Un-created where nothingness is lost in the Bosom of the Father, where the Spirit pronounces with our lips: Abba-Father.
> Then our soul is the soul of Jesus.
> It is no longer we who live; it is Christ, *truly*, who lives in us.[27]

In the last sentence, Chiara emphasizes the word "truly." This emphasis describes the experience that the nothingness spoken about is not the whole story, because God himself fills this nothingness.

God calls us to a communion with him which is a sharing in the very communion of the Son, of Jesus, with the Father. Unity—as is affirmed in the preceding chapter of this book—is the orientation of human beings and the whole of creation toward the Father, in the way that Jesus was always turned toward

---

26. *P'49*, 41, 8 December 1949.
27. *P'49*, 42-44, 8 December 1949.

his Father. "Being Jesus," allowing—as the excerpt says—Christ to live in us, means placing ourselves in this truth.

It was on the basis of that perspective that a way of looking at things to do with both heavenly and earthly realities opened up for Chiara and those with her who formed the Soul that special summer. The text goes on:

> Then within the Bosom of the Father we come to know all the inhabitants of heaven and we understand the work God does in us, clothing us bit by bit in the divine.
> And this was what God revealed this summer.
> The one Soul, of the two of us and of the many united to us, and present in each of us—because united and if united—having arrived inside the Bosom of the Father, came to know the Word, and so it was.
> The Soul had the clear impression of being immersed in the sun. It saw sun everywhere: beneath, above, about, and it awaited new illuminations to accustom its eye to discern all who were living there.
> And it came to know that the Word was the expression of the Father within himself, and it understood that it had been made Church in order to love him.
> And so the Word wedded the Soul in mystical marriage.
> The Soul saw itself as a little group of souls united in an infinite abyss of love."[28]

The Word espoused the Soul. In this extremely concise manner, Chiara describes the experience of that moment that then became the basis for the whole "journey in paradise," as she called it, the basis that runs beneath all the stages of that special period. Strong as it is, the image of marriage is not unusual in Christian mysticism, and is often used in the New

---

28. *P'49*, 45-51, 8 December 1949.

Testament when speaking of the Church called the spouse of Christ (Eph 5; Rev 21).

Communion with God is experienced by Chiara and her group as so real and overwhelming, a flood of light and love, that it can only be described adequately by the image of marriage. In marriage all goods become goods held in common. The Word gives the Soul his own relationship with the Father. Later on in Paradise '49 the image of marriage appears again. It's not intended as a sentimental expression; it's referring to real life, life that comes from putting the Word into practice.

> To live the reality of the marriage of my Soul with the Word—"love," who I saw in paradise after the Father (infinite love), I have to be only *Word of God*. Every instant I live the Word is a kiss upon the mouth of Jesus, that mouth which spoke only words of life.[29]

In order to welcome this gift, the Soul was "made Church." Again, in a very concise manner, the text indicates a fundamental understanding of what the word "Church" means. It is humanity in its openness to God, lived in love. In Paradise '49, this dimension of the Church-humanity often bears the name Mary, referring to the role Mary has in the history of salvation.

We must also say something about a quite unusual expression found in the first paragraph of the text quoted from December 1949. The experience of entering the Bosom of the Father uses the image of the point of a needle, something extremely small, the passageway between the nothingness and the all of God. The two rays—symbolizing human persons turned toward God—"make a pact of unity, becoming Trinity." The word "trinitization," used by Chiara in Paradise '49 on a few occasions, is an expression coined by her to express an experience

---

29. *P'49*, 195-196, 24 July 1949.

that she cannot describe in normal language. Unity is understood well only if it is seen in the light of the Trinity, of a God who is in himself a communion of love. He is one precisely in being distinct within himself: Father, Son, and Holy Spirit, each of whom is the one God, the all, but only by being with the others, in reciprocity, to the point of mutual immanence. That is why "loving is to love and be loved: it is the Trinity."[30]

According to Christian faith, this divine communion has opened up to the human race with the coming of Christ. Every single person can enter into that "marriage" with God, into that communion between the human being and God where one gives one's own nothingness and receives the all of God. Jesus gives us the possibility of sharing in his own relationship with the Father, a relationship that is extended to relationships between human beings, in the community which is the body of Christ. That is what happened in that summer. Those with Chiara who together formed the Soul, and using the image of marriage, "*because of Jesus among them*, have been wedded to one another and are Church."[31] The Church in its deepest reality is the life of the Trinity among human beings where they become sharers in one another's lives, and it then embraces the whole of creation as well.

The new word "*trinitization*" can be understood in this way: "… because of the pact of unity we are one, we are the Soul, but each of us, in becoming distinct, is Soul, each of us is the Soul. We are, that is, patterned on the Trinity."[32]

Through the gift of unity, in Jesus and through Jesus, each one carries the other within themselves. So it can be understood why Chiara, in various explanatory footnotes on the Paradise '49 text, uses the expression "in a trinitarian way" when talking about human relations lived in love.

---

30. *P'49*, 910, November 1949.
31. *P'49*, 203, 24 July 1949.
32. *P'49*, 41, note 50.

This expression should not be read using the category of "model," as if we could orient ourselves to a divine model and imitate it according to our own limited possibilities. That would risk ending up being a poor caricature, destined to fail. The expression indicates rather the openness of the human person who welcomes in faith the gift of God and lives it in mutual love, a love that of course then includes much personal effort. In a footnote comment on this sentence, Chiara says:

> This nuptial reality is without doubt an essential characteristic of the human being created in the image and likeness of God, that is, in that unity, patterned on the Trinity, which is realized also in earthly nuptiality, and which will remain in its deepest essence in eternity. Generally speaking I do not see so much the individual as being in the image of God, but in two people united as are the Father and the Son.[33]

If Chiara uses elsewhere the expression "loving like in the Trinity" when referring to human relationships, it is used in the context of people who, in communion with Jesus Forsaken, have become pure acceptance of the gift of love, not "boasting" of the presence of God within them, or claiming to be able to love to this point on their own strengths: "absolutely empty of ourselves, even of God in us (and this is loving à la Trinity!)."[34] A human person therefore becomes an open door to heaven for others.

The audacious expressions just quoted alert us to the need to be prudent in reading and interpreting the texts of Paradise '49 (as is generally the case with mystical texts). Any direct application of this trinitarian language to human realities risks rendering them banal. The experience of the Soul is an experience "in the Bosom of the Father," of a "place" which is

---

33. *P'49*, 203, note 198.
34. *P'49*, 765, 10 October 1949.

simply not of this world. And yet, the experience can lead to an original understanding of human realities, realities that always retain their own dynamics and their own dignity. The search for the right language for this is a challenge that needs to be worked out in the various fields of knowledge.

1950 and the Transition to Everyday Life

We may ask ourselves: is this experience of one Soul, abiding in a multiplicity of persons and within each one of them, an exceptional experience lived by a small group in that particular period of time, or is it something that can have an impact on everyday life? How can this experience be understood, not as a distant ideal model, but as something to be discovered as a style of life to adopt, bearing similar fruits? Chiara posed this question to herself when after 20 September 1949 she returned to Rome from the Dolomites, where the experience had started, and was immersed once again in the normality of daily life. Some texts, in particular from 1950, part of the Paradise of '49, offer some answers. The following text was written on 27 March 1950, at Ostia, a coastal town near Rome, where Chiara was living at that time with her focolare community:

> We take as the starting point loving God with all our heart, all our soul, all our strength and hence our neighbor as ourselves; therefore we begin to become holy by becoming holy with the others, in communion with our brother or sister, and do not even imagine the possibility of becoming holy individually (because it is absurd). Therefore, at the basis is unity and with unity perfect charity and therefore being perfect as is the Father.[35]

---

35. *P'49*, 1125, 27 March 1950.

Nothing different about this, you could say, when considered in the light of the clear decision to become saints together, in mutual love, a decision that had animated Chiara and her companions ever since 1944 in Trent. What follows, however, shows the depth of the experience of the summer of '49, now translated into a daily spiritual journey:

> Jesus is among us and with him the Holy Spirit who fills us with his seven gifts, at the same time as we, doing the will of God, develop all the virtues. A contemporaneous action takes place on God's side and on ours in the work within us of becoming holy. The gift weds the corresponding virtue in such a way that it is one with it and is distinct from it, as in Jesus, God-who-is-human, the human part was perfectly united with the divine.
>
> This unity of the human part and of the divine part makes us a God-who-is-human by participation. All of us together are a single God-who-is-human like a Sacred Host; distinct we are many who are God-who-is-human (of course by participation), like many fragments of Sacred Host, equal among them and each equal to the whole Host, just as the whole Host is equal to each fragment.[36]

These are surprising and strong words but a basis for them and explanation of them can be found in what St. Paul says of the Church community: it is the "body of Christ," and as such has Christ himself as its ultimate subject and participates in his divine-human nature. The image of the sacred host refers, as in St. Paul, to the root of unity in the community, which is in

---

36. *P'49*, 1126-1128, 27 March 1950. Apart from its relevance here, the text quoted contains other important elements for the spiritual journey that cannot be dealt with here.

the Eucharist (1 Cor 10:17), but it is also the explanatory key for the simultaneity of unity and multiplicity.

Here it is important to clarify that the affirmation that we are "equal" means equality of value and equal participation in the divine life; it does not mean "equal" in the sense of all being the same. The first part of that text, dated 27 March 1950, recounts an experience of the group at that time that in certain ways is also paradigmatic of the unity that can be experienced in Jesus. What emerges is that there was great diversity among them and yet, paradoxically, there was also a full unity among them all.

Chiara tells of a simple moment of communion lived by the first focolarini. On the basis of having declared mutual love they had a "moment of truth." This is a practice which, along with others, would emerge more in the life of the members of the Movement as a help for each person to be shaped by the presence of Jesus within her/him, and so develop their truest and deepest personality. As Chiara wrote in 1948, "there is no charity without truth, because charity is 'truth incarnate'."[37] In the "moment of truth," out of charity, the truth of what needs to be corrected in one another is said, and at the same time, again and always with charity, what gets pointed out is the truth of that "virtue," or better, that special unrepeatable gift that each one brings to the shared journey to holiness.[38] As the following text says, in "the moment of truth," you experience what happens when we "are consummated in one," when we give and receive from one another without reserve and give space to Jesus among us, who makes us one and distinct at the same time. Chiara writes:

---

37. From the letter of 23 October 1948 to Fr. Raffaele Massimei already quoted, in Chiara Lubich, *Early Letters*, p. 83.

38. It is not by chance that even in moments of relaxation in that period at Tonadico where they ought to have been resting, in a game of comparison with someone in scripture, or a flower, etc., they brought out the specific contribution of each one.

Having finished the hour of truth, we could conclude by saying: Jesus among us is: zealous like Graziella, prudent like Giosi, full of light like Pasquale,
loving like Foco, temperate like Marina, affectionate
like Lia, supernatural like Antonio, simple like Mari-
no, affable like Giulio, warm like Giorgio, childlike
like Liliana, strong like Gisella, and so on…

We, the more we are consummated in one, the more
we shall acquire the other's virtue (*"omnia mea tua
sunt"* [all that is mine is yours]), in such a way that
we will be one, each the other, each Jesus. We will be
many persons who are equal, but distinct, because
the virtues in us will be clad in the characteristic
virtue forming our personality.

We will mirror the Trinity where the Father is distinct from the Son and the Spirit, even though
within himself he contains both Son and Spirit.

The same is true of the Spirit, who contains within himself both Father and Son, and of the Son
who contains within himself both Father and
Holy Spirit.[39]

What this text from 1950 indicates is that what Chiara and
her companions lived in the summer of 1949, as a highpoint
of a communitarian mystical life, can indeed imbue our daily
experience. But there is a condition: that in the commitment
to become holy together we help one another to pass constantly
from what the apostle Paul calls the "former self" to the "new
self," our true personality that emerges fully and in a genuine
way when it is grafted onto God, and on this basis, we are
"conummated in one."[40] What then happens is that, in Jesus,

---

39. *P'49*, 1118, 1121-1123, 27 March 1950.
40. See also the explanation given in correspondence by Chiara on p. 63: "When
can two souls be consummated in unity? When they are 'alive,' stripped of
their human side, of their personality and through the Word of Life lived,

we become sharers in one another's lives and carry the others within us. And all of this happens without canceling our distinctiveness. Quite the opposite, it actually helps it grow.

Fundamental in the text we have just read is the affirmation that "we will all be one, each one the other, each one Jesus. We will be many persons, equal yet distinct, because our virtues will be clothed with the characteristic virtue that will form our personality." We can understand what Chiara said at the beginning of the month, "Whoever lives in God is one with everybody and everything and from everybody is *distinct*."[41]

The unity that Paradise '49 speaks about does not cancel out the singularity or the specific dignity of each person, but rather strengthens it as a gift for the others. Each human person, as was seen in the first part of this book, is one of the infinite expressions of God, one of his "words," one of the "tones" with which he utters "love." This is the ultimate basis for the uniqueness of each human person. At the same time, since it is an expression of love, it can only be itself in the gift of self and in relationship with others. Chiara wrote on 8 November 1950:

> Today I understood that each of us, in our place, can have no substitute. We were called by God *to be him...* to be, thus, living Words of life. And the call of God the Father is irrevocable like the Son... God therefore has called us to put on a Word of God which because it is love, is complete, but it also needs another Word to give rise to a new beauty of love. Each one therefore has the kingdom of God within on the condition, however, of losing it moment by moment in each brother or sister, because love is made in such a way that it has what it loses.

---

incarnated, they become LIVING WORDS."
41. *P'49*, 1109, 4 March 1950.

> We therefore have no substitute in the place where
> God has put us. For us, for each of us, the Word of
> life is the clothing, the wedding dress of our soul
> who is the bride of Christ. . . . For us our habit is all
> within: it is our "Habit," that is, our special virtue,
> our strength, our characteristic.[42]

For Chiara, all of this has a strong basis in experience. During
her stay at Fiera di Primiero in the Dolomites in the summer of
1950, among the first focolarini, men and women, the profiles
of some of them stood out in a particular way. Chiara spoke of
the "designs" that they personified, destined to play a lasting
role in the shape and the practical realization of the various
aspects of the Focolare Movement. For example, Chiara saw in
Pasquale Foresi[43] a special grace for everything concerning the
incarnation of the charism of unity, while in Igino Giordani
she saw the personification of the opening out of the charism
to the whole of humanity.

Unity as Chiara experienced it in Paradise '49 does not
flatten the specific characteristics of different people nor make
them uniform. Rather, it purifies them, opens them out to others, and brings them to a fuller realization. Unity is a continual
uniting and distinguishing, and if lived in the right way, it helps
avoid self-absorption and enables each person to be increasingly
an expression of the multiform richness of unity. In one of the
first pages of Paradise '49 Chiara writes:

> In heaven we will be solely Word of God, and in
> the unity among our souls will be the harmony of
> the new song which is the Gospel formed by the
> Mystical Body of Christ. Each one of us will be a

---

42. *P'49*, 1599, 1601-1602, 8 November 1950.
43. Pasquale Foresi (1929-2015) was one of the first focolarini and the first to be
    ordained as a priest, in 1954. Chiara always saw in him a particular role in
    the development of the Focolare Movement and for this reason, as with Igino
    Giordani, considered them as co-founders.

word, but, since each word is the whole Word, each one of us will be the Word, will be a harmony = *a unity*. The new song is the harmony of harmonies! The song of the Trinity. [44]

If what happened in the summer of 1949 served the purpose of experiencing this in a way that was extra-ordinary, what they experienced in 1950 was more a projection of the extra-ordinary into ordinary, normal everyday life, made up of daily encounters within a work of God that is part of the Church and open to the whole world. And it became an experience of Church understood in a broad sense, because it was an experience of how humanity can be renewed starting from God the Father who is the origin and destiny of the creation. It's no surprise, then, that in a writing from 1961, Chiara ends her account of the experience of 1949-1950 as follows:

> And I remember the last "vision" was this: all those Heavens that we had seen and lived and possessed as if they were the most sacred—tremendously sacred—thing, as a result of an intervention like a new dimension, disappeared. But it was not a matter of being extinguished, but of being *sublimated*, because each one of us felt that he or she bore in himself or herself distinctly that which until that moment had been our common heritage. And we came down from Fiera [di Primiero] with this treasure in our heart.

---

44. *P'49*, 82, 20 July 1949.

4.– United in the Name of Jesus.
Unity and Nothingness in Interpersonal Relationships in Christ

by Brendan Leahy and Judith Povilus

The truest expression of unity among people is intimately linked, in Chiara Lubich's thought, to a particular presence of Christ, one that is indicated in Matthew's Gospel with the words, "Where two or three are gathered in my name, I am there among them" (Mt 18:20). Indeed, from the early years of the Focolare Movement, Chiara and her companions often spoke of that presence using the shorthand expression: "Jesus in the midst." A reflection on this presence is the subject of a profound text Chiara wrote in 1950, a text that will form the main focus of our considerations in this chapter. What we propose is to explore some elements of what Chiara means when she speaks of "Jesus in the midst" in reference to Matthew 18:20.[1]

Nowadays it is common to hear it said in the liturgy or at the beginning of a gathering of Christians: "Jesus is here among us because we are united in his name." We should remember, however, that eighty years ago, when the Focolare Movement was born, such a phrase was practically unknown in the Catholic world and, what's more, was feared as dangerous. It was thought that such a statement could be misinterpreted and distract from

---

1. With regard to the exegesis of the gospel passage and other writings on the theological and philosophical implications of Lubich's text, see the related sources: Judith Povilus, *United in His Name. Jesus in Our Midst in the Experience and Thought of Chiara Lubich*, New York 1992; T.J. Surlis, *The Presence of the Risen Christ in the Community of Disciples: An Examination of the Ecclesiological Significance of Matthew 18: 20*, Rome 2011, in particular pp. 369-375. For a recent anthology of writings and conversations pertinent to this theme, see Chiara Lubich, *Jesus in Our Midst: The Essence of Every Relationship*, Judith Povilus, Donato Falmi (eds.), New York 2019.

the sacramental and institutional dimensions of the Church. Chiara Lubich, on the other hand, from the earliest times of the Focolare Movement, found the reality expressed in Mt 18: 20 to be a pivotal point of the spirituality of unity emerging from the experience of the Gospel she was living with her companions in Trent after the Second World War. For his part, Yves Congar considered Mt 18:20 to be *the* expression-synthesis of the Second Vatican Council, whose documents are all imbued with the theme of unity.[2]

When Chiara Lubich speaks of the risen Christ in the midst of his followers, it is clear to her that this refers, on the one hand, to a *free gift* that the risen one makes of his presence. He is alive and wants to be present to us in every point on earth. On the other hand, however, it is up to us to *respond* to the gift and open our hearts, minds, and lives to him. Therefore, in the text under consideration, when Chiara explains that Jesus is among us if we are united in his name, she is referring to two dimensions: a "mystical" dimension, referring to the gift of God, and an "ascetical" one, referring to the commitment that is required of persons who wish to be united in Christ. These two aspects are intimately interconnected in the dynamic of love that characterizes life lived with Jesus in the midst.

In this chapter, we will limit ourselves to reflecting on the second dimension, that is, the "ascetical" aspect that has to do with our openness to the presence of Jesus among us. If the mystical dimension can be experienced as gift through its effects, such as joy, peace, ardor, and new strength, the ascetical dimension is expressed in the dynamics of interpersonal love that are necessary in order to make room for the gift of his presence to be experienced. In Chiara Lubich's view, an "ascetical" adhering to the gift, already given through the death and

---

2. See Yves Congar, "The Conciliar structure or regime of the Church," *Concilium* 167 (1983), 3–9. See also Klaus Hemmerle, "L'Unità nel Vaticano II. I: L'emergenza del tema negli scritti conciliari," in *Gen's* 15 (1985) 11, pp. 6-10, and "L'Unità nel Vaticano II. II: "Alcune dimensioni dell'unità nel pensiero conciliare," in *Gen's* 15 (1985) 12, pp. 5-9.

resurrection of Christ, is required. She outlines a well-articulated process involved in "receiving" and living the gift.

In various passages of the Paradise '49 text, in what might seem at first sight a surprisingly strong way, Chiara affirms that in order to enjoy among us the presence of the risen Lord who is light and life, a "death" is required, a renunciation of one's self, necessary in order to "consume ourselves into one" with others out of love. This means forgetting of oneself, "losing everything."[3] Chiara goes so far as to say that in living love between persons one must be "nothing." This is a word that, as we shall see, is not intended to have a negative meaning but rather, in the light of Jesus Forsaken is to be understood in terms of living what elsewhere she describes as a "nothingness of love."[4] For Chiara there is a close link between unity, Jesus in the midst, and the dying to oneself involved in living an "emptiness of self" in interpersonal relations.

In this article, we are looking at a number of questions: what does Chiara mean when, in explaining the reality of Jesus in the midst, she refers to "becoming nothing" out of love, dying to ourselves, in loving of others? Is it really necessary to love one's neighbor to such an extreme? How can we live this in a way that, rather than ending up being crushed, we find ourselves fulfilled? We offer this reflection also in order to avoid the pitfalls of a false interpretation of the spirituality proposed by Chiara Lubich. As will be shown, for Chiara,

---

3. See later in this chapter. This conviction is present in Chiara Lubich's thought from her early descriptions of the new spirituality: "Mutual love does not mean sentimental feelings. It means the constant sacrifice of everything of myself so that I can live the life of my neighbor. It is perfect self-denial.... Our neighbor was our penance, our mortification, because loving the other required the complete death of our ego."

4. "Living him [Jesus Forsaken meant living the nothingness of ourselves, so all of us were for God (in his will) and for the others" (*P'49*, 11). The theme of "nothingness" in the Christian spiritual tradition is vast. For the meaning of nothingness in Chiara Lubich in the framework of a synthesis of traditional paths see Fabio Ciardi, "Come vivere il 'nulla-tutto' dell'amore," in *Nuova Umanità* 32 (2010) 188, pp. 185-215.

personal fulfillment comes about through a dynamic that is centered on love. Ultimately it is grounded on a desire for life. What Chiara wants to highlight is both an asceticism of love and a mystical life that is both personal and communitarian.

A Robust Requirement of Love, Within the Reach of All

At this point, we shall transcribe in full the main text to which we refer. In the writings of Paradise '49, it is labeled as "undated," but in the final edited version of these writings it is located between texts dated April and May 1950. Presumably, therefore, it was written in the period in which, after the strong experience of a mystical nature in Tonadico, Chiara was continuing to live an intense life of unity in the focolare communities of Trent and Rome. In the light of what she had "seen" and lived during the previous summer, Chiara clarified some of the dynamics of life with Jesus in the midst:

> To be united in the name of Jesus means both to be united for him—that is, to carry out his command (his will)—and to be united as he wants.
>
> When, therefore, we unite even for good purposes, even for religious ones, but which are not in his name, he is not among us. For example: if I unite with a friend in the name of friendship or to do some task or to seek amusement, Jesus is not among us. If I were a religious and were united with a confrere in order to go on some particular mission, Jesus is still not among us.
>
> Jesus is among us when we are united in him, in his will, which means, then, in him;and his will is that we love one another as he has loved us.

This word of Jesus: "Where two or more are united in my name, there am I in the midst of them" is to be commented upon via another: "Love one another *as* I have loved you." (Only God can comment upon God; for this reason only the Church, which has the *Holy Spirit*, can interpret the Gospel.)

Therefore the two of us, for example, are united in the name of Jesus, if we love one another as he has loved us.

Now, from this you will understand how even those of us who live in the focolare do not always have Jesus among us. For this to be so, it would be necessary that in every moment I love you (supposing just the two of us were living in focolare) as he has loved us and that you love me back *in the same way*. He has loved us to the point of dying for us and, still more, of suffering his forsakenness.

Not always, or rarely, does love for our brother or sister require such sacrifice, but if that love which I ought to bear for you (that act which is the expression of love) does not have behind it *intentionally* the way of loving by which he loved us, I do not love like him. If you do not do the same, you too do not love like this, so we are *not* united in his name and Jesus is *not* among us.

You see therefore that for him to be there, it is necessary to love like this. But you know that to love like this means being "another Jesus." Now, for him to be among us, it is necessary before to be him.

But it is a before that is also an after. And here lies a mystery extremely easy to be lived but higher than rational.

In fact, we are not perfectly him until he is among us....

> In practice we realize when he is among us: when
> we feel free, one, full of light—when torrents of
> living water gush from deep within us. [5]

The text is rich and stimulating. It begins with some examples
of being together that, according to Chiara, are not sufficient
to evoke the presence of Jesus in the midst. At times, to best
explain a concept, it can be useful to clarify what it is not. In
this text Chiara mentions various instances when people come
together but there is *not* the essential attitude required for Jesus
to be experienced as present among them in a tangible living way.
This shows clearly that she understands the reality in question
to be *very* demanding. Indeed, the resolve to perform some
good work together is not enough, nor a feeling of friendship
nor a simple readiness to help one another.

The love that is required on all sides is radical love, with
the measure of Christ who gave his life, dying on the cross,
lowering himself, emptying himself to the point of experiencing
the abandonment of the Father, giving himself completely for
the benefit of humankind and the world (Phil 2:7):

> Not always, or rarely, does love for our brother or
> sister require such sacrifice, but if that love which I
> ought to bear for you (that act which is the expres-
> sion of love) does not have behind it *intentionally*
> the way of loving by which he loved us, I do not
> love like him. If you do not do the same, you too
> do not love like this, so we are *not* united in his
> name and Jesus is *not* among us.

The message, therefore, is centered on love, on the love which
is agape, i.e., total gift of self, which constitutes the heart of

---

5. *P'49*, 1230-1242, no date. In this text, and afterwards, italics correspond to
underlining in Chiara's original text. The biblical citations have been transcribed in the form in which they appear in the original text.

the Christian message and which must be mutual in order for Jesus to be in the midst.

A question may arise here: is this reference to agape limited to Christians? In recent years, since the Second Vatican Council, there has been a growing awareness that those who do not yet know Christ can be disposed, by the grace of the Holy Spirit working in their conscience, to love their neighbor with the extreme measure of self-giving, "as" he did. By the power of the Spirit, they are introduced into that current of life which is born of Jesus Christ and which, in his death and resurrection, has reached every human being.[6] Following their conscience well, they find in boundless love their own fulfillment as human persons. The message of the passage we are considering, therefore, has universal application, that is, it is valid for all people of good will. The radical nature of the gift required is a call to which everyone can respond by the grace of God.[7]

Living Nothingness in Order to Have Jesus Among Us. False Interpretations

At this point, with a view to clarifying what is and what is not important for experiencing the presence of Jesus among us, it might be useful to broaden our line of thought and explore some examples of possible deviations—both on a personal level and on a community level—when it comes to understanding what "dying to self," that is, living "nothingness," means in relation

---

6. See *Gaudium et spes*, 22.

7. For further study on the anthropological dimension according to which living love in its ex-static, dynamic movement of going out of oneself and encountering the other is generative of new life in self and in society, we refer to AA.VV., *Risurrezione di Roma. Dialoghi interdisciplinari su città, persona e relazioni a partire da un testo di Chiara Lubich*, Hubertus Blaumeiser, Anna Maria Rossi (eds.), Rome 2017, pp. 163-174.

to letting Jesus live among us in our relationships and to how we build unity. In order to have Jesus in our midst, we need to move within a balanced perspective of true love. This means not watering down what is demanded of us, not compromising, but being aware that the requisite "nothingness" is in view of bringing out the "whole." It is not only the "whole" of unity but also the fullness of our personality that emerges from the presence of Jesus among us.[8]

For some people, the dying to self that is inherent in being ready to give one's life for others could be confused with an attitude that is really more about their own personal negative self-image. This would be the case of those who think: "My ideas don't count; I'm inferior to others, so the best thing to do is to 'make myself one,' that is, to follow what the others say." In this case, the becoming nothing stems from an inferiority complex—whether on a personal, social, or cultural level—and does not help to overcome this complex. There would be a great risk of ultimately feeling humiliated by the dynamics of the community and perhaps simply giving one's assent in order not to lose the affection of the other or others. And since one would never really be expressing oneself, one would end up feeling oppressed. At the risk of overstating a point, we could in this context also think of a false image of Mary as a model of "nothingness," that is, one who does not speak, who lives only passively, in a life without contrasts. But that would be an unhealthy image of subordination, which in some cultures risks promoting subordination of women to men.

Another limited understanding of being "empty of self" arises when there's a negative form of "group thinking." If

---

8. For positive considerations from the perspective of psychology, see A. Partini, OFM, "Un amore integrale nella vita consacrata," in *Unità e Carismi* 17 (2007) 2, pp. 18-25. The author emphasizes how, in order to live a mature love, it is necessary to take into account "also our unconscious motivations, our individual dynamics, and our interpersonal and community dynamics, the objectives we strive for as well as the concrete situations of persons and structures."

individualism is the tendency to prioritize the rights and interests of individuals at the expense of the common good, then "group thinking" in a negative sense moves in the opposite direction. It's the tendency to give priority to the interests and needs of the group. On the one hand, good group dynamics may be directed toward achieving a common commitment to a project, for which everyone gives up their own ideas in order to find a least common denominator. The driving motives would be primarily practical with methods of group animation helping us to feel good. On the other hand, the dynamic of community discernment in Christ goes beyond a mere group dynamic. It requires attentiveness to the voice of the Holy Spirit within. In saying this, we do not want to deny the valid contributions of techniques offered by human sciences such as psychology, but the point is that we must never forget that the source of unity in Christ is "*theo*-logical" and therefore requires the presence of the virtues of faith, hope, and agape.

The "nothingness" of which Chiara speaks should not be interpreted as simply an automatic identifying with the other or with a group. There could be a risk, in group contexts, of idealizing a particular person, to whom one always answers yes. This can be a very detrimental mechanism, both on an individual level and, above all, on a group level. It is important to emphasize that in building unity, living the nothingness of oneself never implies going against one's moral or religious convictions. One must always listen to the voice of conscience, which should never be neglected.

It would also be a mistake to think of "nothingness"/ "dying to oneself" in the life of unity as a listless or non-committal attitude toward life. Living "nothingness" does not mean doing nothing! It does not mean settling for a life of mediocrity, avoiding a life of true commitment to building unity. Dying to self is not equivalent to settling for a peaceful life with little vitality and initiative. Chiara strongly emphasizes that we cannot be parasites of unity, that is, enjoy its fruits without personal commitment. We are called to live a passiveness of love, in the sense of being open to receive our neighbor. But such passiveness is fully active in the sense of giving one's all in order to make room for Jesus in the midst who brings unity.

If listless passivity is an erroneous interpretation of living nothingness, we must be careful to avoid the opposite extreme, namely, a "dying to self" that leads to excessive activism. In never wanting to focus on oneself and thinking that by doing this one is living "nothingness," one easily ends up incurring the risk of nonstop activism, not paying attention to a healthy balance of the various aspects of life, and ultimately suffering a burnout.

Those who have what we might call a "Manichean" approach in life (a third-century A.D. sect of Persian origin that held there's an absolute opposition between the spiritual [good] and material [evil], with corporeality seen as inferior and to be denied) readily identify "dying to self" with the idea that whatever is human is corrupt and so to be rejected. With such an attitude, "making oneself nothing" is interpreted as denying the human dimension in the life of unity. Those who live this way repress creativity, struggle to live an embodied life of unity, and tend toward spiritualism. They fail to appreciate the human dimension of the person in all its various aspects, including the affective sphere. In a religious community, the person in charge must always see to it that there be a correct balance between the various dimensions of life.

It is always important to ask oneself and verify whether the "nothingness" lived in the life of unity brings inner joy. It is a negative sign if one does not experience an interior joy in the gift of self. It means that perhaps the "dying to self" is seen and lived as a crushing obligation, an oppressive demand, rather than a liberating opportunity. Being united should never be reduced to loyalty to an ideology, or to a system of ideas, even if they are beautiful and organized. Unity is about following the living Christ, in a way that is ever new and never sterile. Loving "as" Jesus loved certainly involves a conquest, given that our desire to give ourselves to others is tainted by the inevitable limits inherent in our creaturely condition, but it leads to the experience of a new dimension of inner freedom, an ever-fuller realization of our humanity. One feels "free, one, full of light," as Chiara puts it. One gradually comes to perceive a "spontaneity" in loving, a finding oneself at ease, which is the fruit both of the gift from on high and of personal commitment.

In considering the dynamics of being united in the name of Jesus, the theme of liberating mercy should not be forgotten. When someone has an ideology of perfect unity (never attainable in a complete and definitive way!), tensions are created within oneself and with others, because expectations can arise around how to "live nothingness" or to "die to oneself" while forgetting about mercy and freedom. In this context, it is important to be vigilant to avoid the risk of an abuse of spiritual power over consciences. In the life of unity, if poorly understood, there could be a danger that someone (perhaps with their own fixed idea of what unity means, an idea not open to the newness that Christ, alive now, desires) may "demand" that the other "make themselves nothing" in order to "create unity." We must never forget the liberating power of mercy. Living "nothingness" has to always be a simple invitation on the part of those who want it and a free and willing gift on the part of those who are corresponding in unity. Living the reality of Jesus in the midst is impossible without a *free choice*. It is this very freedom that differentiates the life with Jesus in the midst from situations of inter-relatedness in which we find forms of repression stemming from *internal or external constraint.*

As a final point, we can note the danger of forgetting that "dying to self" in order to love one's neighbor is not to be experienced solely as a human effort of self-denial. This would be interpreting the asceticism that Chiara proposes in a Pelagian key (everything depends only on us).[9] Instead, it is

---

9. Regarding the risk of neo-Pelagianism which assumes that salvation can be

important to keep in mind that in order to live the life of the Trinity (Jn 17:21), which for Chiara Lubich is the ultimate source of unity, one must always give priority to divine grace. The "nothingness of self" coincides with "Christ in self," as we shall see later. If one does not rely on divine assistance, unity can be reduced to an act of strenuous training. In such a case, given one's inevitable limitations and failures, one would end up being frustrated or feeling very discouraged.

A Positive Approach to the Ascetic Radical Nature of Love

What we have just explored, albeit in broad brush strokes, are some of the dangers of a false way of understanding unity among persons. They are all real dangers or aberrations that would make us want to say, "Not death, but fulfillment is what we want!" As the parable of the talents makes clear, God wants us to bring the gifts he has given us to fruition (Mt 25:14-30). On the other hand, the main text we have quoted above, and many others written by Chiara Lubich, leave no room for doubt. What is required, at least as an intentional background, is of an extremely radical nature: to be ready to give one's life out of love involves death and life at the same time, death to our small "self," still tethered by a thousand bonds of self-affirmation, and in its place giving life to Christ in oneself.

---

obtained by individual strength alone, in the *Placuit Deo* letter from the Congregation for the Doctrine of the Faith to the bishops of the Catholic Church on certain aspects of Christian salvation (22 February 2018) we read in note 9: "According to the Pelagian heresy, which developed during the fifth century around Pelagius, the human person, in order to fulfill God's commandments and be saved, needs grace only as an external aid to his freedom (as a way of light, example, or strength), but not as a radical healing and regeneration of freedom, without prior merit, so that he can do good and reach eternal life."

As we have already noted, for Chiara "dying to self" takes place in the act of loving, going out of self. It is in the radical nature of love that one arrives at the fulfillment of one's truest self, in joy and freedom. This is the "death to self" through love required of every Christian. Let us recall the words of Jesus recorded in the fourth Gospel: "Unless a grain of wheat falls into the earth and dies, it remains just a single grain…" (Jn 12:24) or again in Lk 9:24: "Those who lose their life… will save it." St. Paul exhorts us to have, in our interpersonal relationships, "the same mind" as Christ who "emptied himself" (Phil 2:5-7). In this vein, Chiara, like other founders (think, for example, of Saint Francis), urges us to live the Gospel to the letter, without watering it down.

In her approach, Chiara emphasizes the positive that is at the heart of an understanding of love as a gift of self. One comes to be empty or dead to oneself not so much through an act of self-denial as, rather, through a giving of oneself in a radical way: loving God and loving one's brothers and sisters to the point of living "outside oneself perpetually: like a lunatic,"[10] to the point of losing oneself. "We achieve deaths like these," writes Chiara, "above all by loving, by making God's will ours and loving others."[11] To love one's neighbor it is necessary to be ready to give everything, and also to know how to be a gift in opening up to receive others in a total way, being a blank sheet of paper, a "nothingness" in this sense on which others can write.[12]

Chiara describes the dynamic of love as "making ourselves one" with the other/others, that is, identifying ourselves with them, as far as possible. "True love, making oneself one with another, always requires our being nothing, that is, our

---

10. *P'49*, 616, 8 September 1949.
11. *P'49*, 255, note 239.
12. *P'49*, 540, 28 August 1949.

not being in order to be the other."[13] "Whoever lives in the brother or sister... is *nothing*," because such a one is "all and only love."[14] Living our neighbor is the royal road because "in loving our brother or sister, in making ourselves one with them, we find the possibility of denying ourselves, of no longer being there, hence of no longer feeling the burden of our humanity."[15] While, on the one hand, being projected out of oneself in love "demands being utterly heroic," on the other hand "it bestows an immense freedom, a perfect joy."[16]

In the preceding lines we have quoted some sentences of Chiara Lubich taken from other parts of the Paradise '49 text and from Chiara's comments on these texts. They are expressions that reveal the radical nature of the love required in order to experience unity. This unity is a fruit of the presence of Jesus in our midst, as described in the main passage upon which we are commenting. What emerges from these writings is that there is a fundamental link between the "positive" death that occurs in the loving gift of self and new life in Christ. The late bishop and theologian Klaus Hemmerle commented on all this as follows:

> The way to be able to live with him, the living one, is to walk the way of love to the point of death. We can be in unison with Jesus as in a symphony, in unison with the one who is present in our midst, by handing ourselves over to him in a radical way, up to the point of the cross.... In this way, the "as" expressed in the new commandment takes on great significance and becomes a way to arrive at the presence of Jesus in our midst: "Love one another as I have loved you." The presence of Jesus in our

13. *P'49*, 1237, note 893.
14. *P'49*, 612, 8 September 1949 and note 521.
15. *P'49*, 1059, note 800.
16. *P'49*, 1105, note 832.

midst is a presence that passes through the death of Jesus. His dying becomes the strength and measure of our love for one another; it is transformed into our full adherence to God's will.[17]

Bishop Hemmerle's words remind us of how we are called to live the highest measure of love, the measure of Christ himself who died on the cross. The ascetical praxis of those who want to open themselves to receive the presence of Jesus in their midst finds its foundation on the mystery of the crucified and risen Lord, on that Jesus Forsaken whom Chiara discovered as the key to unity. This is a very rich theme, central to unity, as we have already seen in the chapter entitled "The Roots of Unity," and it deserves a fuller in-depth study that we cannot go into here. It is by looking at him that Chiara sees as possible, and so proposes, a readiness to put oneself aside in the interest of others, dying every day to one's own views, one's own reasoning, one's own security, in order to respond with generosity to the demands of love for God and neighbor and so be born anew each day.

The Realization of One's Personality

At this point we might ask, where does one's personality end up in all of this? Isn't there a danger that it could get canceled in a negative way, as we can see happening, for example, in some cases of religious sects, where there is a demand of a "total merging" of the subject into an ideology, even causing psychological damage? Certainly, there is always a risk. It would be, however a misrep-

---

17. Klaus Hemmerle, *Wegmarken der Einheit,* in Ecumenical School of Ottmaring, 1987-1988 (manuscript for internal use), p. 60; Italian translation, cited in Wilfried Hagemann, *Klaus Hemmerle. Innamorato della Parola di Dio,* Rome 2013, p. 276.

resentation, as we mentioned above, a distortion of the radical nature of the love required by the Gospel. True, Jesus demands everything ("those who lose their life for my sake…," Mt 16: 25), and it is not possible to be "half-dead"; death is a totalizing word. However, in this dynamic, if lived correctly, one does not experience being crushed, but on the contrary one experiences a personal elevation. To rise to a higher level, one must leave behind the previous one and in this way arrive at life in abundance.

In a page of her diary Chiara writes:

> Christianity would have us be dead in a certain sense and alive in another, dead to ourselves and alive to the life of God in us; dead to our limited, rebellious, disordered will and alive to a superior will that sets the design of our life into that of humanity as a whole, as a human-divine work of art.

She concludes: "Mortification meaning a kind of halfway repression is not okay. What is okay is mortification meaning total renunciation of an inferior life for a superior one."[18] By coming out of oneself, by "losing" one's own life, one acquires the maximum value of his or her personhood on a higher level. In the same act with which one loses one's personality, one finds it again, strengthened and sublimated. As the Gospel says, we "will find it."

Chiara Lubich was always a strong supporter of the importance of the personal identity of every individual. She specifies, however, that the true personality of each person is Christ in him or her, Christ "clothed"—so to speak—with the particular "idea" that God had when he created us. "My true self" is "that Word of God which 'ab aeterno' God has uttered."[19] Therefore, "we saw clearly that each of us has an utterly distinct, unmistakable personality": it is "the word that God has spoken in

---

18. Diary, 13 January 1972.
19. *P'49*, 244, 25 July 1949.

creating us. . . . That specific word expressed the supernatural personality of each, which the life of the Ideal, with Jesus in the midst, brings to light and empowers."[20] Noting the way in which this supernatural personality characterizes every individual in a unique and decisive way, Chiara commented: "... the Christ in me, which is my true personality, is utterly different from the Christ in St. Catherine, from the Christ in St. Francis or in any other person," and she went on to conclude that "it is necessary that each of us should be ourselves." But myself, yourself, as she noted previously in the same quotation, is Christ in us: "We, losing 'our' personality, take on Christ's, which is much stronger, much more distinct."[21]

Full human realization lies therefore in our being another Christ, participants in his life with our individual personality, characteristics, and temperament. This conviction that our very humanity is strengthened to the extent that we immerse ourselves in the divine, though present in Christian tradition, has emerged more explicitly only in the last century. This is thanks in part to the impact on faith of sciences such as psychology and personalist philosophy. A recent document on Christian anthropology promulgated by the Anglican–Orthodox Ecumenical Commission states, "We grow, not according to an obedience imposed moralistically, but through gladness and love evoked and given freely. We are called to change and grow in grace and faith, to become more Christ-like."[22] It is a concept we also find mentioned explicitly by Pope Francis in his apostolic exhortation *Gaudete et Exsultate* regarding holiness: "Holiness does not make you less human, since it is an encounter between your weakness and the power of God's grace" (n. 34). "It will take away none of your energy, vitality or joy. On the contrary,

---

20. *P'49*, 1045, note 787.

21. *P'49*, 244, note 229.

22. "In the Image and Likeness of God: A Hope-Filled Anthropology," The Buffalo Statement agreed by the International Commission for Anglican-Orthodox Theological Dialogue, 22 (Anglican Consultative Council, London 2015).

you will become what the Father had in mind when he created you, and you will be faithful to your deepest self" (n. 32).

A Personal and Communal Ascetic Dimension, a Mysticism of the New Commandment

Up to this point, in commenting on Chiara's text, we have not yet given sufficient attention to the emphasis she placed on the role of *mutual* love in the dynamic that leads to the presence of Jesus in the midst, a presence that leads to the fulfillment of the human person. Every person is called to live the gift of oneself as the way to his or her own fulfillment, but for Chiara Lubich it is particularly through "consuming ourselves in one" with our brother or sister, lived *reciprocally* between two or more, and through the grace of unity, that one experiences a fuller realization of one's humanity.

In losing, in leaving aside what we consider to be our own, in order to be open and receive into ourselves whoever it is we are with, we acquire the virtues of our brothers and sisters. At the same time, by loving, and particularly in the mutual love that gives life to the presence of Jesus in the midst, we find our own personality strengthened in a "divine mode," so to speak, made more fully participant in the life of Christ. As we saw in the previous chapter, Chiara explains:

> We, the more we are consummated in one, the more we shall acquire the other's virtue..., in such a way that we will all be *one*, each the other, each Jesus. We will be many persons who are equal, but distinct, because the virtues in us will be clad in the characteristic virtue forming our personality.[23]

---

23. *P'49*, 1121, 27 March 1950.

Therefore, one's own personality, with its characteristic talents and gifts, is exalted and elevated in communion with others and by the presence of Christ, so that it is Christ who loves with my heart, thinks with my intelligence, builds a bridge, programs a computer, and so on. One rejoices in experiencing like St. Paul that "it is no longer I who live, but it is Christ who lives in me" (Gal 2:20).

The expression to be "consummated in one," which appears in the text we have just quoted, is significant for the theme we are dealing with because it is also indicative of the extreme degree of love in question. Clearly, with this expression, as we can understand from exploring other passages written by her in the same period, Chiara is referring to Jesus' last prayer, reported in the Gospel of John: "… that they may be one even as we are one, I in them and you in me, that they may be consummated in unity" (Jn 17:23).[24]

Chiara is well aware that the unity of which she is speaking is a divine gift and that is why Jesus asks for it as a gift from the Father. In another passage she says that it is Jesus himself who, like a divine fire, consumes several souls into one soul, his own. Yet such a gift demands a concomitant ascetic effort on our part: to consume ourselves together into one with love. Chiara writes:

> We understood that being consummated in one. . . .
> we were no longer ourselves, but he in us: he the
> divine fire who consummated our two very different
> souls into a third soul: his own: all fire.[25]

Therefore, being "consummated in one" and "being consummated in one" by the fire of Christ are like two faces of the

---

24. This is the translation as transcribed by Chiara, in use at the time. The New Revised Standard Version reads: "… that they may be one as we are one, I in them and you in me, that they may become completely one" (Jn 17:22-23).

25. *P'49*, 384-385, August 1949.

same reality, two dimensions—ascetic and mystical—that in the spirituality proposed by Chiara Lubich are never separated.

With this inter-connection of loving one another and the real presence of Christ among people, we can see a new form of mysticism emerging, one that Chiara calls "the mysticism of the new commandment." It is a balanced mysticism that strengthens each one's humanity in the twofold sense of *being love* and *being another Christ*. By freely loving one another and living as consummated in one, each person finds his or herself inserted in a more lively fashion into the mystical body of Christ. And this, Chiara says,

> ... is balance, light and clarity, normality, the human being in perfection, God humanized... because here everything is in circulation and everything is beautiful and simple like the course of the stars in heaven, ordered like nature, healthy because it is God; with souls who go therefore in all senses toward goodness, toward the good, to health, also physical, because this is the Gospel. . . . And it is because when God circulates, everything circulates, everything is given and we have what we lose.[26]

Conclusion

Everyone feels, even if sometimes unconsciously, a longing for the joy, freedom, and true peace that come from unity. In the main text quoted in this chapter, Chiara states that when Jesus is among us we experience these gifts. In explaining how to open ourselves to the presence of Jesus among us, she says she is convinced that the words of the Gospel, "where two

---

26. *P'49*, 1532, 29 September 1950.

or three are gathered in my name, I am there among them" should be commented on with the other gospel passage: "Love one another as I have loved you." Furthermore, she specifies that the measure of this mutual love is that indicated by Jesus Forsaken on the cross. But how is this extreme measure of love to be interpreted concretely? After having seen some false interpretations that should be avoided, we have highlighted the eminently positive dimension of "dying to self" that Chiara proposes, positive because her perspective is love, going out of self as a gift for others, to build unity. It is a dynamic never to be lived simply as personal asceticism, but rather linked to the liberating and unifying presence of Jesus in the midst and thus to the intrinsically communitarian dimension of the spirituality of unity.

5.– Freedom and Obedience in the Dynamics of Unity

by Anna Maria Rossi and Hubertus Blaumeiser

Before we delve into the theme of freedom and obedience in the dynamics of unity, we would like to make one or two short points by way of introduction. It is clear that modernity has valued and continues to value freedom very highly. Culture and art, human sciences and law, ethics and politics all celebrate in their way the value of freedom. Slavery in various forms has gradually disappeared. The dignity of the human person with his or her fundamental rights has been affirmed and forms of subordination have been opposed in the name of self-determination and emancipation. Society has embraced the concept of tolerance, while the economy has been profoundly influenced by liberalism. By re-engaging with the experience of ancient Greece, democracy has made its way into politics. All of this presents a context in which there appears to be no room for the value of "obedience," perceived in general as an obsolete and questionable reality, in contrast to that of freedom.

In our day, however, we are also witnessing a crisis of democracy and the resurgence of sovereignism and authoritarianism. As a result of neo-liberalism, new forms, not only of inequality but also of exploitation and slavery, are growing. In the name of freedom, individualism, loneliness, and the fragmentation of society have become rampant. In practice, ever since the moment of their birth, the noble ideals of freedom, equality, and fraternity proclaimed by the French Revolution have turned out to be very frail, and indeed in their concrete realization there have been some very serious and even bloodthirsty failures. All of this calls for further reflection.

When we read the Bible we see that, starting with the book of Genesis, freedom and obedience go hand in hand. God created the human being "in his own image" and placed them at the apex of all creation as a free "you" vis-à-vis God (Gn 1:27-28). At the same time, he placed a limit on humanity: " You may freely eat of every tree of the garden; but of the tree of the knowledge of good and evil you shall not eat, for in the day that you eat of it you shall die." (Gn 2:16-17). This limit, however, is viewed by the serpent, the tempter, as something to be surpassed in order to become "like gods, knowing good from evil" (Gn 3:5).[1] The effect of this apparent act of "freedom" ends up, however, notoriously quite different: the relationship with God, the relationship between man and woman, and the relationship of harmony with creation are all broken (Gn 3:8-24).

As we know, the story of the origins of humanity, as presented in the book of Genesis, isn't meant to be a historiographical chronicle of events but rather an account outlining important anthropological truths. And so we find that one of the fundamental themes that will run right throughout the Bible is announced in these first pages, a theme to do with the very question of our happiness and unhappiness in life, not only on a personal level but also on a collective one. Indeed, what is Israel's long journey through the desert after the years of slavery in Egypt, if not an experience of *liberation*, even if it is characterized by ever new disasters that arise from disobedience to the "Law," the rule of life given by God to his people? An experience that centuries later was repeated with the dramatic destruction of Jerusalem and the deportation to Babylon.

Against this background, the New Testament speaks of Jesus' filial obedience to the Father: "Here I am, I have come… to do your will, God" (Heb 10:7, 9; Ps 40:8). And the author

---

1. In reality this promise on the part of the serpent that they would become "like gods" involved a misleading and falsified image of God, as if God indifferently associated with good and evil. In the biblical revelation, however, being like God consists in the gift of self and in the capacity for otherness: in love.

of the letter to the Hebrews specifies: "Although he was a Son, he learned obedience through what he suffered" (Heb 5: 8). Similarly, the Gospel of Luke presents Mary of Nazareth to us as the "servant of the Lord," who replies to the challenging announcement of the angel: "let it be with me according to your word" (Lk 1:38). Both surrender their own will to that of another, of God, with apparent passivity. Yet, in their words there is the presence of an "I": "I come" and of a "here I am," signs of a conscious and personal choice.

The radicalism of this freely lived obedience is manifested in particular in the prayer of Jesus in Gethsemane: "Abba, Father, for you all things are possible; remove this cup from me; yet, not what I want, but what you want" (Mk 14:36). Filial obedience which, according to the well-known Christological hymn of the letter to the Philippians, reached "to accepting death, even death on a cross" (Phil 2:8).

But there is more. Jesus manifests his freedom, and at the same time his readiness to obey, in serving not only God but also others: "For the son of man came not to be served but to serve, and to give his life as a ransom for many" (Mk 10:45). We read in the fourth Gospel. "No one takes it from me, but I lay it down of my own accord. I have power to lay it down, and I have power to take it up again" (Jn 10:18). Washing the feet of his disciples, he invited them to do the same (Jn 13:14).

For the apostle Paul, too, freedom and obedience are a fundamental theme. Especially in the letter to the Galatians, he resolutely defends freedom from the rules of the Law observed by obligation: "For freedom Christ has set us free. Stand firm, therefore, and do not submit again to a yoke of slavery" (Gal 5:1). But this should not be misunderstood: "do not use your freedom as an opportunity for self-indulgence, but through love become slaves to one another" (Gal 5:13). Words that Martin Luther, in his *Treatise on Christian Liberty*, translated with the paradoxical statement: "A Christian is the most free lord of all, and subject to none; a Christian is the most dutiful servant of all and subject to everyone."[2]

The same letter to the Galatians shows how all this also has concrete social implications: "There is no longer Jew or Greek, there is no longer slave or free, there is no longer male and female; for all of you are one in Christ Jesus" (Gal 3:28).

It must be recognized that, conditioned by historical and cultural factors, Christian spirituality and ecclesiastical organization over the centuries have not been able to fully realize this promise of freedom and equality of the children of God, especially since the fourth century when Christianity became the state religion, and the Church, in analogy with civil society and according to the Ptolemaic vision of the world in spheres, became shaped in an increasingly pyramidal way. Indeed, in theology after the Council of Trent (1545-1563) the Church was described as a "perfect society of unequals," in which the predominant dynamic of relationships is from "top" to "bottom." Something similar occurred in religious and consecrated life, where creaturely and filial obedience toward God was accompanied by obedience to a "superior." When not understood well, this entailed the risk of forms of authoritarianism and legalism and, at times, of real abuses of power and conscience. At the same time, also thanks to the charisms of the founders, the Church was gifted with ever new forms of genuine evangelical fraternity (Francis of Assisi) and of cenacle-type circularity (Dominic of Guzmán, Teresa of Avila).

It is against this background that the Second Vatican Council elaborated its ecclesiology of communion, whose implications are increasingly to be understood.

---

2. Beginning of the Treatise *Concerning Christian Liberty.* See *Concerning Christian Liberty* by Martin Luther (1520), Part 2, Translation by R. S. Grignon, The Five-Foot Shelf of Books, "The Harvard Classics," New York 1910, Volume 36, p. 7.

Having made this premise, we will now look at some texts of Paradise '49, which can shed light on how Chiara Lubich conceived freedom and obedience in the dynamic of unity.

From Obedience to Unity

The text with which we shall begin can be considered the entrance into the experience of Paradise '49. This is the story of the pact of unity[3] that Chiara Lubich made on 16 July 1949 with Igino Giordani, a well-known Catholic writer and politician, whom she met on 17 September 1948, in the parliament building in Rome.

The words of this young woman produced in Giordani the conviction that he had found, in the ideal she proposed, not only the answer to his personal aspirations for holiness but also the solution to the social, moral and cultural drama that characterized that era in Italy and Europe of post-war reconstruction.[4] He felt drawn to follow this new light: "I place myself at your disposal: tell me what to do, if I can be useful." Shortly later he wrote to Chiara, "Consider me as the least of the members—of the brothers."[5]

As can be seen from his writings, from the 1920s onward Giordani was fascinated by Saint Catherine (1347-1380), the young mystic from Siena to whom both ecclesiastics and politicians of the time looked to for advice and guidance.

---

3. What we are saying here in regard to the theme of freedom and obedience is building on what Stefan Tobler wrote about the pact of unity in the first part of this book (pp. 44 to 49).

4. S. Cataldi, A.M. Manenti, E. Merli, *Figure femminili nel percorso spirituale di Igino Giordani*, in S. Cataldi, P. Siniscalco (eds.), *Verso un'estate di luce. La cornice storica dell'esperienza mistica di Chiara Lubich nel 1949*, Rome 2019, pp. 103-131, especially pp. 127-131.

5. Ibid., p. 129. An autobiographical account of this meeting and of the impact that it had on Giordani is found in Igino Giordani, *Memorie d'un Cristiano ingenuo*, Rome 2005, pp. 148-153.

Let's come now to the events of 15 to 16 July 1949. The account of these events, written by Chiara on 8 April 1986, forms the premise for the text of Paradise '49 put together in 1991.[6] They interest us because they go straight to the theme of obedience and even transcend it, as we will see, in favor of a "better bond," which is the key to interpreting everything that Paradise '49 can tell us about the theme of freedom and obedience. Chiara recounts:

> Throughout his life Foco, who had a deep love for St. Catherine, had sought a virgin he could follow. And now he had the impression of having found her among us. One day, therefore, he suggested something: to make a vow of obedience to me, believing that in doing so he would be obeying God. He added that like this we could become saints as did St. Francis de Sales and St. Jane de Chantal.
> I did not understand at that moment either the reason for obedience or this two-person unity. The Movement did not yet exist and there was not much talk among us of vows. And I did not understand a two-person unity because I felt called to live "*all* be one."[7]

Right from the beginning, two different horizons of understanding emerge: the proposal of a vow of obedience and unity between "all," which goes beyond not only obedience and its configuration in a vow, but also beyond the idea of a unity limited to two.[8] The text continues:

---

6. For an analysis of the text see Maria Caterina Atzori, *Il Patto in Paradiso '49* (19-37). Historically, the oldest version recounting the pact of unity is the one that dates back to August 1949 (*P'49*, 384-403). A second version was written on 8 December 1949, and in December 1990 Chiara placed it at the beginning of the Paradise '49 text (*P'49*, 38-44).

7. *P'49*, 20-21.

8. Regarding the theme of "spiritual friendships" between two people in the his-

At the same time, however, it seemed to me that Foco was moved by a grace that ought not be lost. And so I said something like this to him: "It may really be that what you feel comes from God. Therefore we ought to consider it. I, though, don't feel this two-person unity because all should be one." And I added: "You know my life: I am nothing. I want to live, indeed, like Jesus Forsaken, who annihilated himself completely. You too are nothing because you live in the same way. So then, we will go to church tomorrow and I will say to Jesus-Eucharist who will come into my heart, as into an empty chalice: 'On the nothingness of me may you seal a pact of unity with Jesus-Eucharist in Foco's heart. And, Jesus, bring about between us that bond which is known to you." Then I added: "And you, Foco, do the same."[9]

Two elements of Chiara's answer masterfully demonstrate what the transition from obedience to unity means:

– First of all, Chiara reverses the roles and places herself in a *relationship of equality and reciprocity* to the point of becoming herself "the obedient one." Despite her reservations, she listens to what Foco asks.

– She does not, however, correspond to it in an acquiescent and passive manner, but introduces a new element to it: in the acceptance of the "other," on the nothingness of herself, she makes room for *the presence of a third: Jesus,* present in the Eucharist, leaving the initiative to act to him.

---

tory of spirituality, and not infrequently between a man and a woman, see Fabio Ciardi, "A founding pact for charismatic communities," in Atzori, *Il Patto del '49 nell'esperienza di Chiara Lubich*, pp. 84-87.

9. *P'49*, 22-26.

Thus obedience in the pyramidal sense gives way to reciprocity between people and to a *common "obedience" to God*, before whom the two of them adopt an attitude of deep listening, letting themselves be molded by his words,[10] and of radical welcome "as in an empty chalice";[11] empty, but specifically a "chalice": capable of containing Jesus and the others. This is perhaps one of the most beautiful images used in Paradise '49 to indicate how our true personality is shaped.

Chiara wrote in a footnote to the text that what emerged was "a better bond than what Foco had wanted. In fact, while in the vow of obedience there is someone who commands and someone who obeys, here we were one through the Eucharist, we were equals, Jesus and Jesus, a single Jesus."[12]

On July 17, when Chiara made the same pact with her companions, she further understood the characteristics of this bond of unity:

> After that I had the impression of seeing in the Bosom of the Father a small troop: it was us…
> In the fire of the Trinity we had been, in fact, so fused into one that I called our company "Soul."
> We were the Soul.

And she observed:

> There were several of us there, but we were one. Each one, then, distinctly was the Soul.[13]

---

10. In the introduction to the Paradise '49 text, Chiara refers to how the pact of unity was preceded by a very intense commitment to living the Word of God to the point of becoming like Jesus forsaken, who had been discovered as "the Word fully unfolded." "All that was needed, therefore, was to live him…. Living him meant living the nothingness of ourselves so all of us were for God (in his will) and for the others" (*P'49*, 10-11).

11. It is essential to understand well the dynamics of nothingness, which in Chiara is always a "nothing that is willed" (*P'49*, 78, note 91), the result of a free choice, not imposed nor endured from outside oneself.

12. *P'49*, 25, note 29.

13. *P'49*, 33, 36 and note 44.

Each one therefore was the whole, part of the whole and hence also part of one another.

We will not dwell further here on this dynamism of "trinitarian" unity, already explored in a previous chapter.[14] We will limit ourselves to simply remembering how this relationship between Chiara and Foco, which was born with the event of the pact and overcame the state of subordination between persons[15] to result in a being equal and being "one" in Jesus, is paradigmatic for the entire experience of Paradise '49 and for the way in which Chiara understood relationships in the life of unity.

It is worth noting that all this took place not in the context of a restricted community, but within the horizon of "all one," and that one of the two protagonists was a politician. This circumstance suggests that what is described here not only has spiritual and religious significance but can also in a certain way affect human life in all its dimensions, including that in the socio-political domain.[16]

Freedom and Obedience in Unity

If we can say that from those pages describing the pact of unity the idea of obedience was superseded by unity, we might ask: So then, does unity replace obedience? And does it replace freedom too? Or is there more to this perspective offered in Paradise '49?

14. "Unity and diversity. The experience of the Soul" (Lucia Abignente, Stefan Tobler, Hubertus Blaumeiser), pp. 63 to 87 of this volume.

15. It should be borne in mind, however, that the Soul has its "center" in the person of Chiara (*P'49*, 36); an aspect which will be dealt with in the chapter of this book, "Chiara Lubich, Mediator of the Charism for Unity" by Fabio Ciardi. What we want to note here is simply that even if there is equality there is an "order."

16. See Atzori, *Il Patto in Paradiso '49*, with contributions from the fields of law, sociology, economics and politics.

In seeking to answer this, we can refer to some passages in the text in which Chiara speaks of paradise and hell. It is no coincidence that her intuitions with regard to these themes date right back to the very first days of that experience of light. We will see how these passages contain not only keys to understanding the afterlife, but they also offer fundamental insights for the here and now in the life of unity and for society itself. What we find in these texts are *two opposing typologies of unity and freedom, obedience and authority.* These texts also indicate how these typologies differ.

In Chiara's vision, the radical opposition between paradise and hell lies in the extreme, vital dynamism of the former and in the rigid immobility of the latter. Since the dawn of civilization, narratives related to paradise and hell have been used by humanity to depict models of an ideal society, proposing paradise as the goal for positive human actions and relationships, and hell as a deterrent for negative ones. In the texts that we will examine, we will see a certain overturning of classical images that led to the conception of paradise as a static model of an equal society having reached its peak. For Chiara, paradise is a place of dynamism, of continuous return to the one, and of an ever-new unfolding in multiplicity, of a unity that is anything but uniformity.

Let's go to the texts. We read in a page from 10 December 1949:

> In Paradise there will be different meetings of souls and from each meeting will come forth the beauty of Jesus. At times among them there will be Jesus strong and generous. At others Jesus meek and humble. And others Jesus all-powerful... It will be an infinite variety that brings about to infinity new blisses of heaven. It will be a savoring of love without ever wearying because always new and delightful. And each vision will be more beautiful than the one

before and the one before will not be disdained
as it is contained in the present and is its cause.[17]

Chiara observed in a footnote to this paragraph: "Therefore, Paradise is always new not just in our relationship with God, but among us." The basic paradigm is not the state of bliss and contemplation alone, but the dynamic and creative encounter between people, in which new facets of one's own personality and that of the others and, ultimately, of Jesus are always manifested (in us, in others, in our midst) or, as Chiara suggests in other texts, of the Word of God through whom everything proceeds from the Father and everything returns to the Father.[18]

Paradise is therefore a place of permanent newness, of maximum freedom. This freedom is not one disconnecting you from others, and much less from the one who is the ultimate origin, the author from whom we come and to whom we can freely return: as diverging rays, projected by the Father outside himself, which re-converge in him[19] or, as Chiara wrote months later, "We are like fires cast forth from the Fire, distinct from the Fire and hence free."[20]

The driving force of this dynamic is love understood as agape.[21] Chiara wrote on 23 July 1949:

> The Father says: "love" in infinite tones and begets
> the Word, who is love, within himself, the Son,
> and the Son, being the Son, echo of the Father, says
> "Love" and returns to the Father!

---

17. *P'49*, 1045, 10 December 1949.
18. Col 1:16: "All things were created through him and for him."
19. See what was developed by Stefan Tobler in pp. 49 to 51 of this volume.
20. *P'49*, 1173, 19 April 1950.
21. Love as *agape* differs from love as *philia* and as *eros*. In the Christian vision agape is conceived as a free gift that has its root in God. From a sociological perspective, the essence of agape, in terms of social relationships, can be identified in an excessive action that creates benefits.

> But all the souls who are in the Bosom of the Father
> (who have arrived there by walking along the exter-
> nal ray, being "Jesus") respond to the echo of the
> Father (= respond to the Father); indeed they too are
> Word of the Father, who responds to the Father…
> Thus the whole of Paradise is a song that rings
> out from every part: "Love, love, love, love,
> love, love…"[22]

What the text, written on 24 July, which we will now look at,
says is that unity and freedom, obedience and authority are
present at the same time, and closely linked to each other, in
this dynamic of love and of the ever-new encounter referred to
in the passages of 23 July and 10 December 1949.

> There Above will be the Idea and the various ideas
> of the same Idea,[23] and therefore there will be unity
> and Trinity (variety). However, (as in the Trinity each
> one is God) each one of the various Ideas will have
> the value of the Idea: it will be God. So in paradise
> there will be the maximum authority, which is the
> Idea of the Father: the Word, which all the Ideas obey
> in their being reduced to him, being him—and there
> is no greater authority than oneself. But there will be
> absolute freedom, because there is no greater freedom
> than obedience to oneself. Freedom then comes from
> the fact that each is not bound to and is *distinct* from

---

22. *P'49*, 101-103, 23 July 1949.

23. It should be borne in mind that when Chiara speaks about "idea" in this and
other texts, she does not mean an abstract idea, but the truest and deepest
reality of every created being. Every creature, and therefore also every human
being, is a "word," or rather an expression, an "idea" of the Father, just as
the Son or the Word is the Idea of the Father, the paramount expression of
the Father.

the other. Freedom is Trinity, multiplicity, variety. And there Above, all is life, all is the Life.[24]

It is impossible to analyze in detail here a text such as this one, so rich in expressive power and depth of intuition, but we will at least try to identify the light it sheds on the key concepts of unity, freedom, authority and obedience:

– *unity* is anything but monolithic. It goes hand in hand with diversity, "multiplicity" (the Trinity), a variety in which each part is also the whole and has the value of the whole;

– *freedom* consists in the fact that each one is "distinct" and "unconstrained" by the other: he or she is not forced either internally or externally;

– *authority* is not extrinsic, formal, juridical, but arises from the relationship with the origin, from the relationship with the Author, in whom the fullness of self is found ("each of the various ideas will have the value of the Idea: it will be God");

– *obedience* is a "reducing" oneself to the one—a bringing oneself back to, relating oneself—to this origin in which one finds the greatest self-realization. It is therefore, an "obeying oneself," one's own "true self," one's most genuine and profound personality.

In the pages where Chiara talks about hell we find the same concepts, but this time described in opposite terms:

– a unity that appears "perfect" but is not, because it is rigid and static, it does not admit variety, it is not able to unite opposites;

– an "anarchic" freedom that is not anchored to its origin (Greek: *archè*) and so ends up being a slave to itself and to things;

---

24. *P'49*, 140-143, 24 July 1949.

– an imposed authority, which does not leave the other free and is not free even in itself;

– a forced but intimately rebellious obedience: it does not want to do what it does.

In the words of the text of 24 July:

Here below people were attached to that which was passing… there below they find again that which is empty and vain and dead and pain and cold and fire, everything that can hurt by burning and freezing, because it will be a cold (gnashing of teeth) that will never unite with fire (eternal fire) and therefore never be lukewarm, since in hell two things can never love one another. There will be all things, but still, immobile… there will also be the one who runs, but never stopping. Either motion alone or quietude alone. Never the unity of opposites, for unity would be life.

And there will be *Unity* alone without there being Unity in Trinity, for down below there will be only authority. There will be Lucifer who all will obey *under constraint*—perfect unity in Hell and utter anarchy because no one wishes to do what they do (including Lucifer who also acts under constraint). And those who did not wish to submit to an authority here below, which would have made them *free* children of God, will be slaves for all eternity.[25]

Authority, obedience, freedom and unity are elements of both realities. What distinguishes paradise from hell is the trinitarian dimension; in other words, it is love, which is ultimately the giving of oneself freely, that making space, that setting oneself

25. *P'49*, 147-148, 24 July 1949.

aside so as to open up to the other, which is indispensable in order to pass from stasis to movement, which is life.

To compose freedom and unity, obedience and authority into one, Chiara looks at the love as she sees it in the life of the triune God, where, despite the apparent inequality of two subjects—the Father who generates and the Son obedient until death (Phil 2: 8)—the dynamism of being continuous reciprocal gift makes them equal in an equality of love:

> In the Bosom of the Father shadow and light will have equal value, for we will think of the Father thinking of the Son in him and of the Son thinking of the Father in him....
>
> Three Reals form the Trinity and yet they are One because Love *is and is not* at the same time, but also when *it is not* it is, because it is love. In fact, if out of love I take something from myself and *give* (I deprive myself—it *is not*), I *have love* (it is).[26]

It should be noted, as emerges from this analogy, that equality is not a leveling out; rather it is being of equal value, enclosed in the diversity proper to each one, which preserves within itself the ability to be a gift for the other. This is a dynamic that enlightens our humanity: the value that each one has in him or herself does not amount to a plus or a minus, nor is diversity annulled. The diversity awaits mutual recognition and realization. Diversity does not generate superiority but becomes a "place" for dialogue, in which the encounter between two identities of equal value, in the gift of self, generates unity.

---

26. *P'49*, 159-160, 24 July 1949.

An Obedience which Generates

Looking at the pact of unity on the one hand and considering the final fulfillment, which is life in paradise, on the other, we found in both a making oneself nothing out of love and a freely chosen and lived-out obedience to authority. But we have also seen that this authority is not a superior and that this obedience consists in the fact that two or more people open themselves up to a third: to Jesus and, in him, to the Father. It is against this background and with this premise that we now ask ourselves about the authentic meaning of the obedience of one person to another.

What has been written up to now is valid to the extent that we are "in the Father's bosom," and we will be there permanently and definitively only in eternal life; a life that, in Jesus, already begins here and now but finds its fulfillment only after death and in the resurrection. How, therefore, we must ask ourselves, in the midst of our human limits and conditionings, can this ideal vision, which will fully come true only in heaven and yet can be anticipated in some way when there is the grace of unity resulting from our mutual love, become tangible in everyday life?

A page written on 29 July 1949 speaks about this. As well as clarifying the relationship between Chiara as founder and those who follow her, it explains the key that enabled her to live total obedience toward ecclesiastical authority;[27] a

---

27. It should be noted that from the very beginning of the Focolare Movement in Trent, the newness of the charism was profoundly connected in Chiara with her undisputed obedience to those who represented the Church for her. See Lucia Abignente, *«Qui c'è il dito di Dio». Carlo de Ferrari e Chiara Lubich: il discernimento di un carisma,* Rome 2017. In his *Letter on the occasion of the funeral of Chiara Lubich,* Benedict XVI noted that, "… the service that Chiara has given to the Church" has been "a silent and incisive service always in harmony with the Church's Magisterium…. This is so because Chiara and her Work of Mary have always sought to respond with docile fidelity to the appeals and desires of each of them [of the popes]. The thought of the pope was for her a sure guide" (18 March 2008).

radical obedience, which was absolutely not passive or servile, but rather *generative*.

The key is the dialogue between Jesus and Mary at the wedding feast of Cana, in which Mary made a request to Jesus, not for herself but for the married couple in difficulty. At first, he harshly rejected it, but then he took it on. Mary's invitation to do "whatever he tells you" hastened the "hour" of Jesus (Jn 2:1-11). Chiara sees, in this scene, the model of a dynamic that leads to "enlarging the heart," of a free love that opens up to the other by choice and not by obligation, an overabundant love that ends up providing a light for the other, building the other up in such a way as to make him or her grow in his or her identity, while at the same time welcoming his or her difference. Here we understand how dialogue, in order to be truly such, requires the parties to come out of themselves, to move their *focus* beyond themselves, to live, in the truest and most normal sense of the term, in an "ecstatic" way. It is a search for the truth that is in us but also outside of us, because it is something greater, beyond us: it is found in the Father.

> She, obedient, submitted herself to the will of the Son, which was an enlargement of her heart, an increase in love, and with this love of hers she (made Jesus), was the Light of Jesus in such a way that he did Mary's will which had become his, that is, the Father's. Jesus, therefore, continually brought his Mother to the "greatness, perfection" of God the Father.
>
> With her he never made *unity* of charity (as we say) *but of truth* and for her this was perfect charity, for he did not adapt himself to her, but he adapted her to himself.
>
> Perhaps now we can comprehend his words "O woman, what have you to do with me?" as meaning, "Remember that between me and you there is

infinity.... Therefore! enter into me and with me
do the Father's will."
Then he performs the miracle requested.[28]

What is striking is the extreme dynamism of this obedience. It is not a person blindly carrying out what is said by a superior, but a welcoming the other in a generative process that brings out what both really tend toward: the will of the Father, which—as Chiara affirms—"says: 'love' in infinite tones."

Jesus makes his mother's will his own, but only *after* having led Mary *in* and *with* him to do the will of the Father. It is not a question of obeying a command, rather of adhering to a project. A relationship made up of *freedom* and *dialogue*: Mary does not fall silent before her son. She expresses herself with freedom in her caring and maternal personality, but she submits to the dimension of Jesus which is of a greater love, and she believes in his power. Their relationship becomes a *going toward the Father together*, the third, the one to focus on, the one to look toward, the one who truly realizes mine and yours: in this way the will of the Father works the miracle awaited by Mary and willed by Jesus. Here, Mary becomes a model of a

---

28. *P'49*, 359-362, 29 July 1949. For our commentary on this page, we are availing of the contributions from two members of the Abba School, Adriana Cosseddu and Gennaro Iorio, respectively for the field of law and that of sociology. We also include the following comment by Alberto Lo Presti, a member of the Abba School for Ethics: "Chiara sees Mary as an ark (container), filled with the Holy Spirit, perfect. But the ark is a finite measure, never able to contain the infinity of God. Mary, who is already perfect, can become still more perfect. At the height of her virtues, she is called to 'expand her heart,' that is, to enlarge the ark, in order to receive more Holy Spirit. Mary is clothed with virtue. Now, however, she is called to a greater wisdom. The process of spiritual growth, in her, therefore, does not have an ethical purpose, it does not aim at making Mary better and more talented, but rather at making her more wise. The challenge is now not virtuous behavior but the truth. For this reason Jesus shows her a relationship of unity in truth. A unity in charity would not help her. On the contrary it would trap her in her humanity, preventing her from going beyond her already good nature to launch herself towards the infinite measure of God's wisdom."

freedom which is expressed not because "I want" but because "I love" (Adriana Cosseddu).

This form of obedience-love that enlightens is what inspires Chiara in the relationship that she feels she must live with the highest authority in the Church: the Pope. It is a relationship which is at the same time free and obedient "until death."[29] In fact, the passage we have quoted ends with these words:

> Perhaps, as Jesus does to Mary, the Church (which is Jesus, the Holy Father) will speak to us, but we, obeying with our death, will illuminate the Pope.[30]

Even if this affirmation refers specifically to the relationship between a particular Work of the Church and the pope as the representative of the Church as a whole, we can nevertheless recognize in it the fundamental dynamic of the experience of love-agape, which transforms the classical conception of command and obedience.

Those who love, those who renounce themselves to live the other, as a choice and not as an obligation, are returned to themselves, to their difference and immutability, that is to their absolute personal uniqueness. The path is always: from oneself to the other, to then return to oneself, renewed. Renouncing oneself is not the final outcome of love, but a stage. The destination is a new reality, which is unique, exactly because it is love. Whoever obeys or commands, following the experience of "making themselves the other," by loving, transforms the forms of command and obedience. Lived in love, obedience becomes generative. This allows us to understand how Chiara can say: "by obeying with death we will illuminate the pope" (Gennaro Iorio).

These pages show us obedience also in its interpersonal dimension. It is motivated by the fact that there are those who

---

29. See Phil 2:8 and Chiara's account of it in *The Cry*, New York 2001.
30. *P'49*, 363, 29 July 1949.

have the grace and the task of representing the whole, of the Church and also of a work of God, and therefore are assisted by the Holy Spirit in a special way. However, this obedience does not nullify the dimension of "trinitarian" reciprocity and is anything but passive. It does not end in "death" to one's own thought and will but re-emerges with an unprecedented contribution to the whole, and in this way it becomes generative.

The Positive Pole and Negative Pole in Unity. Light that Comes from the Night of God

Let's come now to the life of unity in everyday life, as Chiara understands it; a life that, in her vision of things, is not only made up of interpersonal relationships but is "the mysticism... of the new commandment"[31] or, to use an expression of Pope Francis, "mystical fraternity."[32] As such, the life of unity is characterized by a great radicalism, which does not consist in external renunciations but in the ability to make room in oneself for God and for others, or rather, for God who comes to us through others and comes to meet us in others.

How do the values of freedom and obedience interact in this mysticism lived socially and, in this sociality, lived with mystical depth (obedience above all in the etymological sense of listening to the other)? We will now examine this, based on texts from Paradise '49 dating back to the year 1950, that is, to that period when Chiara was translating, as it were, the mystical experience of the summer of 1949 into a spiritual doctrine that would provide light for the personal and community, ecclesial and social life of those who follow the path of unity.

---

31. *P'49*, 1530, 29 September 1950.
32. Pope Francis' Apostolic Exhortation *Evangelii gaudium*, n. 92.

In these passages, we will encounter, on the one hand, a very strong need to welcome the other, and especially those who "come from unity,"[33] to the point of being ready to live a "night of God," that is, to put aside the presence and the light of God as we find them in ourselves, to make room for the others and to seek them in the others. On the other hand, the dimensions (which have already been mentioned) of reciprocity of love and of generative obedience are always present, directed not so much to the other person, but together with them to a third: to God who makes himself present in the encounter between people who live a reality of "nothingness for love" with each other. This is what Chiara expresses with the image of the two poles of electric light, reinterpreting with a communitarian key that *nada* toward God, of which Saint John of the Cross speaks.[34]

But let's start at the beginning. Up to now, we have often affirmed the need to "be nothing" in order to live unity according to what is expressed in Paradise '49. And yet, if you think about it, the deepest yearning of every human person is "to be someone," "to always be more," "to be more and more themselves." This is what is generally sought and is also and above all sought in relationships with others. How can we reconcile this deep and legitimate aspiration with such a demanding endeavor? Isn't losing everything, even God himself, beyond our strength and contrary to our nature? It is with this question that we will now present the following texts of Paradise '49 to try carefully to understand their meaning.

> St. John of the Cross (he, the "doctor of nothingness") teaches us that everything in us is to be ne-

---

33. Who are already part of those who have chosen "unity" as their way of life (editor's note).

34. It should be borne in mind, as various scholars of Christian spirituality have pointed out, that in these passages, it is not Chiara's intention to provide an examination of the doctrine of St. John of the Cross in all its implications, but rather she refers to him in order to further expound on and clarify her own understanding of the Christian life.

gated so that God may enter—and here we have his night of the senses and of the spirit.

Of us Jesus asks something more. He asks also the negation of *God*.

In fact, when we, a small mystical body, love one another so as to let Jesus speak in the one who is the head, we have to negate everything: silence the senses, the intellect, the will and the memory and even the inspirations of God. Everything is to be given to the head who, filled with so much love, overflows with light for all. Hence the head gives everything too. If the head gives God's light, if the head has the capacity, it is because he or she is in the perfect threefold night. Indeed, giving God's Word, the head gives Love, which is the Word's essence.

Our life therefore is Jesus Forsaken. We live, like him, in perfect negation.

And this not only when many of us are gathered together with one who is speaking. But always: when a brother or sister speaks, we have to negate everything (even divine inspirations) so as to enter into our brother or sister perfectly, having made ourselves *nothing* and therefore simple. Only simplicity enters everywhere. And this means being *one*. And here is seen how being one is being Jesus Forsaken.[35]

The model of Jesus Forsaken, the "perfectly negated one," indicated here by Chiara as "our life" and as the way and condition for "being one," is really that darkness, that "night," into which, instinctively, we would not wish to enter, perhaps especially because of our modern sensitivity, when it is suggested that we negate ourselves before a "superior." This immediately seems like an unacceptable form of authoritarianism on the one hand and

---

35. *P'49*, 1129-1133, 3 April 1950.

of servility on the other, even if in our daily lives, we continually experience the need to join social entities such as institutions, aggregations, groups, or work organizations in which an authority, a guide, a leader is part and parcel.

In the encounter with others, is it possible to preserve our freedom and self-realization, and even to discover that these can be enhanced, by negating ourselves? In other words, using Chiara's image, is it possible to enter the night and generate light?

In the passage above, it is clear that only mutual love makes this transition from nothing to everything possible. A love that is a free, gratuitous, complete gift of self opens the relationship with the other up to a dimension of reciprocity and transcendence toward a "third," that fully realizes both the giver and the recipient. It is worth specifying that in this dynamic, the precious component of the personality of each one is important; if lived authentically, each one regains their own personality, not negated but expanded, enhanced.

This is what emerges clearly in a further comparison between the way of unity and what St. John of the Cross proposes. Chiara observed that in the spirituality of the saint, which was of an individual nature, "with his dark night he was the negative pole that, united to God, the positive pole, made the light shine out or spring forth in himself." Chiara then explained how it is in the spirituality of unity:

> . . .We are negative pole and positive pole among brothers and sisters. The one who comes from Unity [i.e., the Movement] (because he or she bears Christ within and so God) is the positive pole; the other, the one loved—if empty and in the proper disposition (in the night)—is the negative pole. The contact between them gives the Light of Jesus among them and hence in both. We truly bring the Kingdom of God on earth. Indeed God is among us, and through us this current of love (which is

the current of Trinitarian love) passes across the
world into all the members of the Mystical Body,
illuminating them all.[36]

The image is powerful and very significant: there is no hierar-
chy between the negative and positive poles; one is not more
important than or superior to the other; they are both equally
necessary and of equal quality. Thus the lack of one determines
the failure also of the other to generate light. Despite their
substantial diversity, they can only contribute together, in their
contact, to give life to something that is neither one nor the
other: the electrical current. Likewise, outside of love, neither
the "superior" nor the one who obeys will have success. Continuously choosing to be a gift of love for one another and at
the same time open to God as the "third" generates a current
of love that enlightens: isn't this perhaps our full realization, as
individuals and as a society?[37]

It should be borne in mind that the positive and negative
parts are not statically linked to certain persons or tasks or
roles. If it is true that whoever represents the whole (of the
Movement, of a community, of a portion of the Church...)
deserves in a special way to be listened to, welcomed, and
obeyed because of a specific gift of the Holy Spirit (the "grace
of office"); on the other hand it is also true that he or she
must negate themselves and live the "night," in order to give
not themselves but God, the light of God, to which we have
opened ourselves up together, in mutual love. But this is not
enough: "always: when a brother or sister speaks, we must
negate everything (even divine inspirations) to enter him or

---

36. *P'49*, 1271, no date.

37. Adriana Cosseddu notes: "Let's think, for a moment, about how coexistence
could change, in a social dimension, with respect to the observance of rules, to
which we are bound as citizens. We could convert the latter from a passive and
formal 'obedience' to the command of the law, into 'adherence' already within
ourselves to a project for the common good, to contribute to a coexistence
where justice, 'guardian of relationships,' becomes the 'foundation' of peace."

her perfectly."[38] In fact, only in this way, Chiara reiterates, is it possible to be "grafted one into another, as are the Persons of the Trinity."[39]

But the horizon of the life of unity is broader: it cannot fail to expand toward the "all one," as we have already seen in the pact. Living an agape-love radically to generate unity among us is the way to unleash a current which, by setting people and things in motion, lets universal fraternity advance day after day.

The Vow of Obedience

The vow of obedience has been a centuries-old tradition in the Church since the beginnings of monasticism. While, on the one hand, at the moment of making the pact with Foco, Chiara did not feel a vow would be an adequate bond between them, nevertheless she did not ignore its value and importance. She kept it and established it as a rule, together with the vows of chastity and poverty, for those who consecrate themselves in the Work of Mary as focolarini.[40]

In Paradise '49 Chiara indicates how to live this commitment: she invites us to transcend it in love, in an overabundant love that is measured on Jesus Forsaken and is a bond that is at the same time more radical, free, deep, and dynamic. It is transcended in the reality opened up in the pact of unity that leads us to live as sons and daughters in the Son and, in him,

---

38. Further on in Paradise '49 Chiara speaks of this reversal of roles and of the newness of life that it produces, in the form of an experience lived with one of the first focolarini: "My soul, therefore, having entered into the paradise of Antonio (into his Jesus), saw all things and persons via that Heaven. . . .In his Heaven, therefore, I colored my soul and my vocation with his Word and I projected it around me, onto those who are mine. . . (*P'49*, 1554 and 1557, 28 October 1950).

39. *P'49*, 1264, no date.

40. For married focolarini, the vow is replaced by a promise.

in the Bosom of the Father. We read in the page written on 25 August 1949:

> Today I ordered my little ones to lose both obedience and command: and only to *love*. And in the place of virtues they will have *God* Love and in him the virtue of obedience which is the Word himself and of governance which is the Father himself.
> To have God we must lose the virtues: *all of them*.
> This too is a secret that has burst from the Wound of Jesus Forsaken.[41]

These are "the virtues that are not manifestly charity," Chiara explained in a note later on. And she continued: "Jesus Forsaken teaches us to be nothing and so one has everything, God, who is Love."

It is not by chance that Chiara described the moment of her consecration with these concise words: "I have married God." In the same way, the vows of the first focolarine were experienced as a "flight into God": a detachment from one's ego, from possessions and from family ties, to get to another dimension, Love with a Capital L: in God, in the Father. With this love, it is a question of fulfilling not only every religious obligation but also every just civil obligation. Where this love fails, the vow of obedience remains as guardian of unity, but the ideal is not the vow, it is not the Law, it is love that leads us to "enlarge our hearts."

Conclusion

At the beginning of this chapter, we recalled how modernity values freedom, noting there have been achievements marking

---

41. *P'49*, 484-485, 25 August 1949.

undeniable progress throughout the journey of history even if with contradictions. Against this background, the value of obedience might seem to be moving in the opposite direction, something almost irreconcilable with freedom or in any case to be limited more than anything else to respect for the rules and the dimension of legality. However, in briefly considering the roots of the Jewish and Christian experience as they are expressed in the biblical texts, we saw how freedom and obedience are intimately correlated as coessential dimensions of love.

Our journey in this chapter through some texts of Paradise '49 has tried to highlight how Chiara Lubich's charism of unity is grafted onto the biblical vision and carries it forward, in faithfulness to the origins. Freedom and obedience are presented in her spiritual doctrine as intrinsic dimensions of the dynamic of agape-love and of unity, which transcends them but at the same time contains them in a purified and stronger way. On the one hand, freedom is understood as the distinction of the human person from God and from others and therefore as a possibility to love God and neighbor, not out of obligation but rather out of free choice. Obedience is lived as adherence to one's own origin and as a filial attitude toward God, but also as acceptance of the other, of Jesus in every person and in particular in those who have the grace to represent him and to represent the whole community.

The condition for authentically living freedom and obedience according to the testimony of Paradise '49 is the emptying of oneself, freely making oneself nothing out of love. This should not be understood as the negation or cancellation of one's personality, but as a supreme act of freedom going beyond the narrow confines of an ego centered on oneself, welcoming the other in oneself and living one's life in terms of sonship and of fraternity in the reciprocity of love: a love that, in the gift of self, becomes generative.

6.– Chiara Lubich
Mediator of a Charism for Unity

by Fabio Ciardi

Perhaps the last historic appearance of the risen Christ was the one to Saul on the way to Damascus.[1] The previous appearances were to the women, to the eleven, and to the disciples, explaining what they should do. But this time the Risen One refers to others: "rise and enter the city and you will be told what you are to do." From then on, the Lord will refer to his Church because, living and present in it, he speaks through it. Ananias is troubled and puzzled, even if, carrying out the task entrusted to him by the Lord, he becomes a minister of his revelation (Acts 9:1–19). The time of the Church and its mediation has begun. From then on, God keeps choosing people as instruments of his word. This is the history of prophecy and charisms accompanying the people of God on its journey. Anthony of the desert, Basil, Augustine, Benedict, Chiara of Assisi, Angela Merici, Teresa of Avila, Vincent de Paul, Teresa of Calcutta, with thousands and thousands of others, are the voice of God throughout the ages. They repeat the words of the Gospel that come alive and real in their lives and their deeds.

The word "unity" too—which we will hear expressed in many shades of meaning in this book—is a word from the Gospel that, continuing the divine logic of ecclesial mediation, is repeated to the Church, through a person, Chiara Lubich.

---

1. Again and again, Paul declares that this was a genuine manifestation of the Risen One (1 Cor 9:1, 15:8; 2 Cor 4:6; Gal 1:16; Phil 3:10).

Unity, the Fruit of a Charism

Chiara's awareness of being the instrument of a gift for the Church was accompanied by the disproportion she recognized between herself and the charism. She focused on the greatness of God and the gratuity of the gift. She says:

> The pen does not know what it will write, the artist's brush does not know what it will paint nor the chisel how the sculptor will use it. And similarly when God takes someone in hand to bring a new work [of God] into being, that person does not know what he will achieve; he is simply an instrument. And that I think is my story.[2]

St. Teresa of Calcutta had the same experience, when, speaking of herself, she said: "I'm like a little pencil in his hands, nothing more. It's he who thinks. It's he who writes. He does everything...."[3] Similarly in our own time, Blessed Giacomo Alberione, when writing of himself, noted: "Don Alberione is the instrument chosen by God for this mission, which has carried out by God, under both the inspiration and the will of God."[4]

For Chiara Lubich, it was very clear her own vocation and mission was "to proclaim" the word "unity"—a proclamation of thought and of life that were to become visible in a work [of God] and in concrete action:

> Whenever we are asked how our spirituality can be defined, and what is the difference between the gift that God has poured out on our Movement

---

2. Michel Pochet, *Stars and Tears: A Conversation with Chiara Lubich,* London 1985, p. 14.

3. Mother Teresa, *The Joy in Loving,* J. Chalika and E. Le Joly (eds.), London 2000, pp. 91–92.

4. *Ut perfectus sit homo Dei. Mese di esercizi spirituali, aprile 1960,* vol. 1, Rome 1960, p. 374.

and the gifts with which he has enriched others in the Church in our times and in the past, we do not hesitate to say: unity. Unity is our specific vocation; unity is what characterizes the Focolare Movement.[5]

Summarizing in a simple but effective way, Chiara intuits how spiritualities can be concentrated around one word and then compares them with that word to grasp what is specific to them:

> ... as "poverty" could be for the Franciscan movement, or "obedience" perhaps for the Jesuits, or "the little way" for those who follow St. Thérèse of Lisieux, or "prayer" for the Carmelite following St. Teresa of Avila, and so on. Unity is the word that summarizes our spirituality.... Unity, therefore, is our ideal and nothing else.[6]

Bound up with the choice of a concrete person, the word "unity" as a summary-word, just as in the case of other gospel words put into practice during the Church's journey, has a history that Chiara Lubich is fond of recalling. In her book, *The Secret of Unity*, having spoken of what's specific to her own vocation, she writes, for example:

> If unity is our typical vocation, let us return for a while to the beginning of our forty-year long history, to when it was set alight like a flame.... Let us recall some things that occurred and read again the written records we have kept about this idea.... Let us go back again to the early days.[7]

5. Chiara Lubich, *The Secret of Unity*, p. 20.
6. Ibid., pp. 20, 37.
7. Ibid., pp. 21–22.

The idea of unity is not only a doctrine but the fruit of what a person has lived, of an experience, and should be understood by locating it within that experience.

This is not the place to go through the journey of Chiara Lubich's understanding of unity. Still, we have to mention how, when the Second World War was raging, and the city of Trent in Northern Italy was being bombed, Chiara with other girls often had to take refuge in a cellar. On one such occasion, by candlelight they were reading chapter 17 of the Gospel of St. John. A new conviction took hold of them—that these words of Jesus' last will and testament were the magna carta of the new life being born around them; together they offered their lives to Jesus in order to be instruments of unity.

A history and a concrete person. In order not to turn her thought on unity into an ideology we have to recall how Chiara Lubich was chosen to be a bearer of a charism; a woman who allowed herself to be drawn into the charism, fully corresponding to it with docility, to the point of becoming its essential component, the charism's inescapable bearer. While the gift is offered to this one person, it is destined for all, which goes with the nature of a charism given "as a service" (1 Cor 12:5)—it is meant for the one who receives it and for the community it reaches, thanks to the mediation of the receiver.

The ecclesial destination of the charism of unity has been recognized repeatedly by pontifical approvals.[8]

---

8. John Paul II, "Message of the XXV Meeting of the Bishops friends of the Focolare Movement," in *L'Osservatore Romano*, 15 February 2001; Hubertus Blaumeiser and Helmut Sievers, eds., *Chiesa-Comunione. Paolo VI e Giovanni Paolo II ai Vescovi amici del Movimento dei Focolari*, Rome 2002, p. 87; John Paul II, "Address to the Bishop Friends of the Focolare Movement," in *L'Osservatore Romano*, 14 February 2003.

Bearer of the Charism of Unity

At the beginning of the experience of Paradise '49 we learn something specific regarding Chiara Lubich's identity. It emerges in conversation leading to the pact of unity between her and Igino Giordani. She says to Igino: "You know my life: I am nothing. I want to live, indeed, like Jesus Forsaken, who annihilated himself completely. You too are nothing because you live in the same way."[9] Notice here Chiara's first definition of herself in Paradise '49 is: "I am nothing." We should never forget how she sees her own "I" as "nothing." We often find this repeated throughout the Paradise '49 text as an interpretative key, as when she writes: "my soul which is nothing in itself."[10] It is a "willed nothing," the fruit of a positive action of conforming herself to Jesus Forsaken who, in love and for love, has given all to the point of complete self-emptying, so that the other may be.[11]

Gradually, as the months went on, and the experience of paradise continued along with a deepening of mystical union, this awareness of her own nothingness not only did not lessen, but Chiara became ever more conscious of God's infinite otherness and so of her own nothingness, a requirement for the identification of her own "I" with Christ's, to the extent

---

9. *P'49*, 24.

10. *P'49*, 78, 20 July 1949.

11. "Yes, it is a nothing that is willed. For I said: 'I am,' but I make myself nothing, that is: 'If there is some good, I make it nothing; if there is an inspiration, I make it nothing; if there is some evil, I make it nothing (I put it into the mercy of God); if I am, I make myself nothing.' It is an act of making-nothing that I do (*P'49*, 78, note 91). In the formulation of the pact, the affirmation of one's own nothingness is accompanied by a strong comparison: "like Jesus Forsaken." In Chiara Lubich's thought the idea of personal "nothingness" is a rich one. On this, I refer to two of my studies: "Sul nulla di noi, Tu," in *Nuova Umanità* 20 (1998) 116, pp. 233–251; "Come vivere il 'nulla-tutto' dell'amore," in *Nuova Umanità* 32 (2010) 188, pp. 185–215.

that—made another Christ—she could say with him the word "Father," at the moment that marked her entry into paradise:

> In fact, that Jesus who was in the tabernacle was also here in me, was me too, was me, identified with him. Therefore, I could not call out to myself. And there I felt coming spontaneously from my lips the word: "Father."

This is a substantial word because uttered in the Son, made Son:

> And in that moment I found myself within the bosom of the Father.[12]

On 24 July 1949, she became aware again of being newly "one with him" (P'49, 197): Christ in her—on her nothingness—is her true "I": "In fact, we are if we are Jesus; otherwise we are nothing. When I entered into paradise I was no longer myself, I was Jesus in me."[13] It is precisely because of this recognition of her "nothingness" that when referring to herself she was not afraid to use bold terms and to speak with a great authority. There is no ambiguity: In expressions like these, Chiara's individual "I" is not confused with the divine "I," rather it is transparent, a "nothingness," in such a way as to be a channel for something infinitely greater. As in biblical tradition, the prophet does not speak his own words, but God's, so she expresses nothing of her own, but only the other.

The next immediate and important passage is from the "I" to the "you." Proposing the pact to Igino Giordani, having declared her own nothingness, she continued by saying: "You too are nothing." And this is the premise for constituting a plural subject, "we" (composed of Chiara's "I" and Giordani's "you," which expands to the "we" composed of the focolarine

---

12. *P'49*, 26.
13. *P'49*, 131, note 146.

who live with them and then of the others who will come), which in the text is often indicated by a single noun, "Anima/ Soul" or "Claritas": the many "souls" constitute "only one Soul," which is all light. Chiara herself notes: "Through the reality of the Soul, in Paradise 'I' always means 'we,' identified with Christ, hence it also means the one Christ."[14] "The one Christ" is a reality that opens to the "plural," as she affirms a year later, when the experience has become well established:

> When we are united and he is there, then we are no longer two but *one*. In fact, what I say is not said by me, but it is I, Jesus, and you in me who say it. And when you speak it is not you, but you, Jesus, and I in you. We are a single Jesus and also distinct: I (with you in me and Jesus), you (with me in you and Jesus), Jesus among us in whom I and you are..[15]

This is confirmed by the novel composite noun "Jesus-we" that we often find in Paradise '49.

In this dynamic of unity and distinction, from the first days of the 1949 experience, Chiara Lubich perceives her own "I" as a unique and unrepeatable reality, like a word uttered by God from all eternity, within the one Word.

> I (the idea of me) is "ab aeterno" [from all eternity] in the mind of God, in the Word; therefore "ab aeterno" I am loved by the Father and "ab aeterno" I hold the place the Father has assigned me. And, that is, my true "I": Christ in me. There Above I am that Word of God which "ab aeterno" God has uttered.[16]

---

14. *P'49*, 488, note 437.
15. *P'49*, 1252, summer of 1950.
16. *P'49*, 244, 25 July 1949.

At the same time she understands the "content" of that Word: "I believe that my Word there Above is '*Ut omnes unum sint*' [May they all be one], that is, 'Unity'."[17] This is the discovery of her own vocation, and at the same time of her own mission, insofar as every vocation is mission. The phrase *ab aeterno* which gives her personal identity also holds for the charism communicated to her and of which she is the bearer.

> This is probably because God, in sending the charism to the earth, has uttered the Word: Unity I have always been aware of this; that is, right from the beginning I felt that the charism expressed in me was "where two or more" (Mt 18:20) and that the light which sprang from it was Jesus in the midst of us.[18]

There are many ways in which Chiara Lubich expresses herself as "I." She certainly has her personal "I" with her unique and unrepeatable individuality as a woman from Trent in Northern Italy with her family and social history, her specific formation. She also experiences herself as an "I," which, by God's grace, finds herself in the Bosom of the Father and traverses a journey of knowledge and identification in the reality of Paradise. She personally also experiences the absorbing "we" of the "Soul/Anima," making of many "one." But in Chiara we can also recognize the "I" of a person chosen as bearer of a life-giving charism for the Church, able to generate a work (of God) that will become the Focolare Movement and spread it throughout the whole of humanity.[19]

---

17. *P'49*, 245. She says this again towards the end of Paradise '49, 2 September 1950 (1498) and also in note 994 referring to this text.

18. *P'49*, 245, note 232.

19. Stefan Tobler, "L'io di Chiara, nel Paradiso '49," in *Nuova Umanità* 43 (2021). These various dimensions of the "I" should be distinguished and at the same time remain intertwined with each other. The analysis of the foundational texts should pay attention to the richness of that identity, requiring great interpretative caution to avoid confusing the various dimensions.

If it is true that from then on she no longer conceives her life as outside the unity God had fashioned by creating the "Soul," it is also true that within this Soul, she has a unique role, of which she is aware: to be its heart, its center. She is the one who in the experience of Paradise '49 "sees" the reality of heaven. By sharing this, she allows all who belong to the Soul to see this with her too, but this is always thanks to her mediation. Already on 26 August she says:

> I (Chiara) am the eyes of Claritas because, as the Father in the Trinity sees in the Son (but the Light does not see itself), I see in my children. The children instead see the reality of their mother one with them.[20]

In this "seeing" she expresses the specific gift of the charism, for which Chiara is aware of having an irreplaceable role:

> I understand that God has given to me alone the light of unity and has shown me—to the point of making me die in an ocean of light (which is rarely understood by others)—in all its vastness the being and law and life of the universe: in its vastness and in its particulars. Now, the others will have it by participation—that is, to the extent they participate in it. And this depends upon me and upon them: I give them Claritas as Jesus did ("and the light you have given me I have given them"[21]), and they will receive it if they want it. Certainly, Wisdom belongs to whoever loves it and therefore desires it.[22]

---

20. *P'49*, 500, 26 August 1949.
21. In a specific note: "Here it refers to the charism of unity" (note 593).
22. *P'49*, 737–738, 1 October 1949.

Months later she explains this again:

> These mysteries took place in me, Chiara, but no
> sooner were they communicated to the rest of the
> Soul than we perceived them to be shared: only that
> I sensed the Christ being formed in me—besides the
> Christ in me—was the Mystical Christ surrounding
> me in the brothers and sisters now completely one
> with me....[23]

The way those belonging to the Focolare Movement live the
charism is by "participation" in the source, which is inseparably
the person of the founder and the gift God has given her. She is
aware of this, as when, already at the final period of her experience, she writes on 8 November 1950: "The focolarine and the
focolarini, in their speaking and their living, give witness to me:
to the Light God has given me."[24] These are words which make
obvious the inseparability of charism and person, although this
is not to be understood as a psychological mechanism by which
the personality of the focolarino is "substituted" for Chiara's,
nor as a negation of the plurality of the gifts of character or
personality, but rather as the illumination or new understanding
of one's own self in a deeper plan of unity. Indeed, in those
very days around November 1950, Chiara also speaks of the
distinct roles developing within the emerging Movement, fo-
cusing on and giving value to the diversity of gifts possessed
by all those who formed the first nucleus of the Movement,
the beginning of a work (of God) that will develop in multiple
ways throughout the years.

    To adhere to the charism remains a free participation. As
we saw in the text of 1 October 1950, with regard to the light of
the charism, Chiara writes: "they will receive it if they want it."

---

23. *P'49*, 340, 10 December 1949.
24. *P'49*, 1595, 8 November 1949.

This kind of relation between founders and their followers is something we find in every kind of foundation of a charismatic group, and is easily documented.[25] Every founder and foundress is an instrument of God, a channel for participation in his grace. Everyone has the freedom to follow his or her own way, but whoever wants to share in the founder's spirituality and charism has to follow that founder in the experience the Spirit has given him or her to live.

To live the charism of unity as it has been given through Chiara Lubich cannot be done without having a personal relationship with her, beyond time and space. Chiara would have been able to repeat what Angela Merici said to her daughters in her *Terzo Ricordo*: Jesus Christ "has chosen me to be the mother, both alive and dead, of this noble company."[26]

An Instrument of Unity

Regarding Chiara Lubich, as with other founders, there have been criticisms of her unique and unrepeatable role within the Movement,[27] that she assumed an authoritarian position that would have blocked others from expressing their own personality. As a result, it is specifically the notion of unity that is questioned. So it is useful to read a page written toward the end of Paradise '49, dated 23 November 1950, that has given rise to misunderstandings.[28] In my opinion, it is the most

---

25. I refer to my first study on this matter, *I fondatori uomini dello Spirito. Per una teologia del charisma di fondatore*, Rome 1982, pp. 312–386.

26. *Tertio Precetto*, in T. Ledóchowska, *Angèle Merici et la Compagnie de Ste-Ursole à la lumière de ses documents*, vol. 1. Rome 1967, p. 263.

27. The Focolare Movement was officially approved by the Roman Catholic Church in 1962 with the name "Work of Mary."

28. See my article, "Unità nel Paradiso '49: alcune osservazioni metodologiche," in *Nuova Umanità* 41 (2019) 233, pp. 113–133.

appropriate description of the role of the foundress within the work of God she generated.

> Every soul that belongs to the focolare has to be an expression of me and nothing else. My Word contains all those of the focolarine and the focolarini. I am all of them in synthesis: I am the head, like Jesus.... When I appear, therefore, they have to let themselves be generated by me, be in communion with me. I too, like Jesus, have to say to them: "Those who eat my flesh…" To live the life that God has given them, they have to be nourished with God who lives in my soul. Their attitude before me must be a *nothingness of love* that calls forth my love. And I then open myself and, speaking, communicate myself to them. They are nothing and hence have no problems; they have already lost their soul because what they are is the living Ideal, a living Jesus Forsaken that is, the "Other," not self. And then I can communicate everything and draw out from deep within myself, that is, from God in me, as much as I can. And the truth is revealed.
>
> I require that those who are mine be perfect like the Father, that they be love actualized and I accept nothing else.
>
> If they are otherwise I forsake them, taking from them even what they believed to have. Like Jesus. Our Unity is Unity therefore, and a single soul must live: *mine*, that is, the soul of Jesus among us who is in me.
>
> These focolarine, who *always act like this*, are perfect. They are Jesus among us with me. Because they have kept nothing (and together with their soul they have lost even their partial inspirations), they have everything.

> With this we are *one* and this One lives in all.
> Whoever does not behave like this and wants to
> keep something back is nothing.[29]

It is helpful to highlight straightaway two phrases that help in our understanding of this text. In the first statement—"My Word contains all those of the focolarine and the focolarini"—Chiara Lubich explains that the kind of relationship asked of all who follow her is to be established on the basis of a charismatic understanding of the Gospel:

> Given that every word of Jesus is truly such because it is contained in his testament, the Word of every focolarina and focolarino must be lost in my Word, which is "ut omnes unum sint [May they all be one]" (Jn 17: 21).[30]

She has understood that her "true I" has been given by the "word" that God has uttered for her from all eternity. Naturally this holds for everyone. For example, a few days before the text we are considering was written, on 8 November, Chiara wrote:

> Today I understood that each of us, in our place, has no substitute. We were called by God *to be him*, not solely to be focolarini: to be, thus, living Words of life.... For us, for each of us, the Word of life is the clothing, the wedding dress of the soul who is the bride of Christ.[31]

So each person has their own "I" that makes each one unique and irreplaceable before God himself, and should remain as such.

A few months before that again, on 16 May 1950, Chiara clearly understood that all the words of the Gospel converged

---

29. *P'49*, 1612–1619, 23 November 1950.

30. *P'49*, 1612, note 1045.

31. *P'49*, 1599 and 1602, 8 November 1950.

on the "testament of Jesus," that is, on the new commandment of reciprocal love and the unity connected with that.

> The rest of the Gospel is entirely at the service of his Testament, and it is intrinsic to his Testament, and so has value only because it shows how to live his Testament.[32]

Just after that she explained:

> The testament of Jesus appeared to us as the Gospel in synthesis. Often we gave this example: let us imagine the Gospel as a plain, a piece of land where all the Gospel words are written; and down below, summing them all up, the testament of Christ. The Lord, in teaching us the unity to which all Gospel truths are linked, has, as it were, made a hole in the ground so that we penetrate and understand the rest of the Gospel from within, grasping it at the root of each word, in its truest sense.[33]

The relation between Chiara Lubich as a person, or of her deepest "I"—given the "word" uttered for her by God, "ut omnes unum sint"—and those who share the charism with her, the multiplicity of people who in their turn are unique and unrepeatable "words," is analogous to that between Jesus' testament and the words of the Gospel. As the gospel words find their full realization in unity, so the persons sharing in the charism of unity find their full realization in living unity, by entering into relationship with the foundress, as a charismatic "word" bearing unity and expressing Jesus' testament.

A second statement has to do with how Chiara communicates her own experience: "The truth is revealed because

---

32. *P'49*, 1297, 16 May 1950.
33. *P'49*, 1297, note 924.

Jesus is in our midst." This is an important comment because it distances itself from the idea of an imposed authoritarianism: truth is communicated exactly in the relation of communion between all the members of the community growing around her, from that presence of Jesus flowing from their unity, where they are all actively co-responsible.

The centrality of unity is not conferred by Chiara Lubich but by Jesus, by associating himself with her, making her another him and the mediatrix of the charism, an instrument of himself. A careful linguistic reading can illustrate this, for which I recall a contribution Anna Maria Rossi offered me. The comparison with Christ is again and again confirmed through repetition of the adverb "like" between "I" and "Jesus": "I am all of them in synthesis: I am the head, like Jesus": "I too, like Jesus, should say to them…": "If they are otherwise I forsake them, taking from them even what they believed to have. Like Jesus." This is emphasized by expressions such as: "Our unity is unity, therefore, and a single soul must live: *mine*, that is, the soul of Jesus among us who is in me"; "These focolarine… are Jesus among us with me." The use of the adverb "like" does not make the comparison in terms of identity (as on the other hand a metaphor would) but associates two distinct elements. In other words, the "like" creates a connection while at the same time preserving the distinction.[34]

It seems clear that Chiara Lubich's use of the pronouns "I," "me" and "we" is in the context of a charism.[35] This suggests a reading of the text in the context of a connection of *relation-communion* rather than of *obedience-command*.

---

34. Anna Maria Rossi, "L'uso della similitudine in Paradiso '49 [1961], in *Come frecciatte di luce. Itinerari linguistichi e letterari nel racconto dal '49 di Chiara Lubich,* Rome 2013, pp. 99–112.

35. See what Maria Caterina Atzori has to say in her essay, "La creatività di Chiara Lubich: *within* and *beyond* the Italian language," in *Il dire è dare. La parola come dono e relazione nel pensiero di Chiara Lubich,* Rome 2017, pp. 91–102, especially pp. 96–99.

Analysis at the semantic level where the words used in that statement belong, leads to the same conclusion (my emphases): "My Word *contains* all those of the focolarine and the focolarini"; "I am all of them in *synthesis*"; "they have to let themselves be *generated* by me, be in *communion* with me"; "they have to be *nourished* with God who lives in my soul." The "me-Christ," subject of the action, appears as the one who contains, generates, nourishes, and therefore gives life. This would lead to the conclusion that basically Chiara is taking the physiognomy of a mother. If this is accepted, even the verbs "I require," "I accept nothing else," and the sentence, "If they are otherwise, *I forsake them, taking from* them even what they believed to have," should be understood as the generative and educative action of a mother, who wishes the good for her children, rather than an exercise of power.[36]

Specific ways of speaking are also often used, along with words belonging to the semantic field of verbal communication which provides an emphasis and particular value. In the text we find "expression," "I have to say to them," "a nothingness of love that calls forth my love," "and I open myself and, speaking, communicate myself to them," "I can communicate everything and draw out from deep within myself, that is from God in me, as much as I can." In Chiara Lubich's thought, "saying is giving," the word—or the communication of the charism—is gift and "creates" the other in a deep relation, generating a reality: it is in this way that every charismatic family in the Church is born. So we find in these paragraphs a demanding request for, and at the same time the complete radicality of the gift of self, which renders evident the unrepeatable and inimitable generative power of the foundress of a work of God.

---

36. How can we forget, even though it stretches the analogy, what Paul does when confronted with a brother with whom he must break off relations (2 Thess 3: 14), or who indeed is "delivered to Satan" (1 Cor 5:1: 5)?

In this saying-generating action carried out by the "subject" *Christ-Claritas*, there follows what we can syntactically designate as the "object-complement," that is, the part that the action is aimed at, in its turn, becomes subject: "These focolarine are Jesus among us with me... We are one and this One lives in all." The focolarine and focolarini too are therefore a subject with the foundress; they do not passively suffer, as it were, her actions but actively carry them out with her, and are essential for her own experience. They are called to full participation in the charism, to a fullness of themselves, and not a limitation (or worse, a substitution) of themselves by Chiara.[37]

In the text of 23 November 1950, unity is understood as the experience of the whole community along with that of each one participating in it. "To become nothing," that is, to enter into the dynamic of complete and reciprocal self-giving, means to receive all from God and this is the experience of all: "Because they have kept nothing (and together with their soul they have lost even their partial inspirations), they have everything."

If the beginning of the text is focused on Chiara Lubich as expression of the Word—the charism—the conclusion is not a passive participation by the others in her interiority or a unity of subjection to her, but the realization of unity in each one: "With this we are one and this One lives in all." The first "one" is not capitalized and can be understood as a relation of love and of unity brought about by people thanks to the gift of

---

37. We have to locate this experience in its correct historic context. The group of people who lived the experience described in Paradise '49 is really heterogenous, as can be seen in the chapter of this book dedicated to the theme of "Unity and Diversity. The Experience of the Soul" (Lucia Abignente, Stefan Tobler, and Hubertus Blaumeiser). The first focolarine were personally very different, each unique in their own way. They come across as people happy to live this experience together. So the writer of the text we are looking at is not worried about a cautious use of language that would avoid misunderstandings, because it is already clear from the reality lived by all that their experience is one of love and joy. This is testified by the first companions' many autobiographies, beginning with Igino Giordani's.

reciprocal self-giving. But this is only the premise for becoming tabernacles in which the "One" (capitalized) can dwell.

Instrument of Unity for Humanity

Chiara Lubich's vocation and mission is not finished in giving life to a work in the Church—the Focolare Movement—rather it goes further; its horizon is the whole world. This universal openness is already there in the first pact with Igino Giordani, when she becomes aware that the bond of unity has a universal significance: *not two one, but all one.*

Hers is a charism that on the one hand established in the Church "a new family of virgin souls born of and called by God to ignite fire in the world and bring unity there," who are "my closest children." On the other hand, Chiara is aware of being called "to help the whole of humanity find its place in Paradise, in the inheritance left me by my Spouse: Jesus Forsaken."[38] As this text shows, Chiara Lubich has a specific role, that of being foundress of the Focolare Movement, along with her awareness of a universal mission because that is the dimension of the *ut omnes.* She gives birth to a work of the Church so that it should be a sign and promotion of its universal vocation. On 6 September 1949 she writes:

> I feel I live in me all the creatures of the world, all the Communion of Saints. Really: because my *I* is *humanity with all the people that were, are, and will be.* I feel and I live this reality: because I feel in my soul both the delight of Heaven and the anguish of humanity that is all a *great Jesus Forsaken....* Jesus is again on earth in me: and all this because I have

---

38. *P'49,* 582, 6 September1949.

entered into the kingdom of heaven (through the famous pact of unity at Primiero). Hence it is he who lives in me: he who delights, he who suffers and my life bears fruit in the redemption of the human race. Thank you, my Jesus! What happiness.[39]

Is this a superhuman claim? Yes, it is the claim of God shared with his creature, and possible because the creature made "Church" is called to share in the mission of Jesus, to the point of being identified with him. It is the fulfillment of the Christian vocation.

These are just a few points regarding the richness Chiara Lubich's understanding of unity is shown to have, and of the mission which God asked of her.

---

39. *P'49*, 582, 6 September 1949.

List of Contributors

The individual chapters of this book have specific authors. Nevertheless, as explained in the Introduction to this book, all members of the Abba School in the years 2014-2020 contributed to the preparation of this volume.

Lucia Abignente (Italy), historian, theologian and in charge of the Study and Historical Research section of the Chiara Lubich Center (Rocca di Papa). She teaches at the Claretian Pontifical Institute of the Consecrated Life at the Lateran University Rome.

Catherine Belzung (France), biologist, lecturer at the University of Tours and a member of the Institut Universitaire de France. She is associate editor of *Frontiers in Behavioral Neuroscience* and a director of the Inserm iBrain Research Institute.

Hubertus Blaumeiser (Germany), theologian, formerly taught at the Gregorian University. He is editor of the *Ekklesía: Pathways of Communion and Dialogue* review. He coordinates the "Ecclesiology-Missiology-Pastoral Theology" group of the Abba School.

Teresa Boi (Italy), pedagogue and teacher. She coordinates the *Education-Unity* (EdU) International Commission.

Francisco Canzani (Uruguay), a lawyer and an ecumenist, is councilmember of the Focolare Movements General Council with regard to the aspect of wisdom and studies. Previously he taught at the Theology faculty of Montevideo (Uruguay).

Fabio Ciardi (Italy), theologian and coordinator of the Abba School during the period 2014-2020. He is a lecturer at the "Claretianum" Theology of Consecrated Life Institute at the Lateran University Rome.

Adriana Cosseddu (Italy), a lawyer and lecturer in penal law at the University of Sassari in the school for specialisation for legal professions. She coordinates the international Communion and Law Commission.

Pasquale Ferrara (Italy), ambassador. At the Sophia University Institute of Loppiano, Florence, he lectures in processes and institutions of political integration. At the LUISS (Rome) he lectures in diplomacy and negotiating.

Anouk Grevin (France) lectures in management at the University of Nantes (France) and at the Sophia University Institute (Loppiano, Florence). She is a member of the international *Economy of Communion* (EdC) Commission.

Claudio Guerrieri (Italy), lecturer in philosophy, history, and the science of education in high schools. He also lectures on the Masters programme in intercultural and interreligious mediation at the Pontifical Salesian University in Rome. Formerly he taught at the Higher Institute for Religious Science at the Pontifical Lateran University.

Marie Thérèse Henderson (Scotland) is a musician and composer and a student of the philosophy of music. She also lectures at the Sophia University Institute (Loppiano, Florence).

Gennaro Iorio (Italy) is a professor of sociology at the University of Salerno and Director of the Department of political and social studies. He is a member of the International Sociological Association and of the editorial committee of *Studi di Sociologia*.

Mervat Kelli (Syria) completed her PhD in the area of patristics, in particular the area of Syro-Orthodox studies. She lectures at the Lateran Pontifical University (Rome) and is a member of the Abba School for Orthodox Theology.

Brendan Leahy (Ireland) is the Catholic Bishop of Limerick and co-Chair of the Irish Inter-Church Meeting. He is a visiting professor at the Sophia University Institute (Loppiano, Florence) and previously professor of Systematic Theology at St. Patrick's College, Maynooth, Ireland.

Alberto lo Presti (Italy) is a political scientist and director of the *Nuova Umanità* review. He lectures in political theory at the Sophia University Institute (Loppiano, Florence) and the history of political doctrines at the Lumsa University in Rome.

Declan O'Byrne (Ireland) is a theologian and lectures at the Sophia University Institute (Loppiano, Florence) and at the Urbaniana Pontifical University (Rome).

Alessandro Partini OFM (Italy), a priest, doctor, and psychologist. He lectures at the Superior Institute for Formators linked to the Gregorian Pontifical University (Rome).

Giovanna Maria Porrino (Italy) is a biblical scholar and lectures both at the Sophia University Institute (Loppiano, Florence) and at the *Mystici Corporis Institute* (Loppiano, Florence and Montet/Broye, Fribourg, Switzerland).

Judith Povilus (USA) is a mathematician and theologian and lecturer in logic and the foundations of mathematics at the Sophia University Institute (Loppiano, Florence).

Anna Maria Rossi (Italy), linguist and Italianist. She teaches literature and is co-ordinator of the "Linguistics-Philology-Literature" group of the Abba School.

Renata Simon (Germany) pursued studies in mathematics, chemistry, and theology. She is a councilmember of the Focolare Movements General Council with regard to the aspect of wisdom and studies.

Callan Slipper (England) is a theologian, with a particular interest in the area of philosophy of religion. He is the National Ecumenical Officer for the Church of England and a member of the Editorial Board of *Claritas: Journal of Dialogue and Culture.*

Stefan Tobler (Switzerland), theologian and professor of Evangelical theology and director of the Institute for Ecumenical Research at the Lucian Blaga University, Sibiu (Romania). He is editor of the *Review of Ecumenical Studies Sibiu.*

Pál Tóth (Hungary), semiologist, lectures at the Sophia University Institute (Loppiano, Florence) and is a member of the international *NetOne* Commission.

FOCOLARE MEDIA

Enkindling the Spirit of Unity

The New City Press book you are holding in your hands is one of the many resources produced by Focolare Media, which is a ministry of the Focolare Movement in North America. The Focolare is a worldwide community of people who feel called to bring about the realization of Jesus' prayer: "That all may be one" (see John 17:21).

Focolare Media wants to be your primary resource for connecting with people, ideas, and practices that build unity. Our mission is to provide content that empowers people to grow spiritually, improve relationships, engage in dialogue, and foster collaboration within the Church and throughout society.

 Visit www.focolaremedia.com to learn more about all of New City Press's books, our award-winning magazine *Living City*, videos, podcasts, events, and free resources.

NEW CITY PRESS